Unbelievable Crimes Volume Eight

Unbelievable Crimes, Volume 8

Daniela Airlie

Published by Daniela Airlie, 2023.

While every precaution has been taken in the preparation of this book, the publisher assumes no responsibility for errors or omissions, or for damages resulting from the use of the information contained herein.

UNBELIEVABLE CRIMES VOLUME EIGHT

First edition. December 14, 2023.

Copyright © 2023 Daniela Airlie.

Written by Daniela Airlie.

Table of Contents

Unbelievable Crimes Volume Eight 1

Introduction 3

Vigilante 5

Genie 13

Pyromaniac 29

The Witch 41

Hangman 51

The Hike 69

Mother 75

Soulless 85

Malicious Matriarch 93

Final Thoughts 109

The right of Daniela Airlie as the publisher and owner of this work has been asserted in accordance with the Copyright, Designs, and Patents Act 1988. No part of this publication may be reproduced in any format without the publisher's prior written consent. This book is for entertainment and informational purposes only.

Although research from various sources has gone into this book, neither the author nor publisher will be held responsible for any inaccuracies. To the best of the knowledge of the author, all information within this publication is factually correct and derived from researching these cases thoroughly. The author may offer speculation and/or opinion about the cases covered throughout this book.

Danielaairlie.carrd.co[1]

---

1. http://danielaairlie.carrd.co

Introduction

Welcome to Volume Eight of Unbelievable Crimes, where the premise of this series - to cover lesser-known crimes - resumes. Many of you reading this will have come from previous volumes, so you already know the focus of these anthologies.

The forthcoming tales are some of the most despicable, depraved, and demented offenses to be recorded in the archives of true crime. From stories of vulnerable children to vengeful teens to the chronicles of simply evil individuals, each case covered in this installment makes you wonder just how immoral and wicked the human race can be.

Certain cases, in particular, highlight that evil can wear the mask of good quite convincingly. No amount of success or likability can change the fact that these people are unhinged and dangerous. Sadly, we often don't find this out until it's far too late.

These select crimes include true-life descriptions of abuse, sexual assault, and violence, so please bear this in mind before continuing.

With that said, when you're ready, let's embark on Unbelievable Crimes Volume Eight.

Vigilante

Leon Gary Plauché, Gary to his friends, made his way through Baton Rouge Metropolitan Airport and found a payphone. He dialed the number of his friend and chatted away, blending in with the other casually dressed 40-somethings who were making calls. Only Gary wasn't like the other men there.

Eventually, he spotted a police entourage escorting a criminal through the busy airport and suddenly hung up the phone. In the middle of the officers was a man named Jeff Doucet, a criminal protected by law enforcement from anybody who would want to harm him.

Gary made his way toward Jeff as inconspicuously as he could and pulled out a gun, shooting the man point-blank in the head. Officers tackled Gary and pinned his revolver to the wall to stop further shots taking place. Medical attention was sought for Jeff, who was bleeding out on the cold airport floor.

You would think that Gary deserved to go to jail for a long time for this crime, which was a clear attempt to kill another man. But Gary had his reasons, and his reasons for wanting to kill Jeff Doucet were condoned by many. This is a rare sentence to type out, but Gary Plauché's attack on Jeff Doucet had him hailed by many as a hero.

The man had committed vile and sickening crimes against Gary's son, Jody. Jeff had gained the boy's trust and molested and raped him, with the abuse only coming to an end when the man was arrested.

This tale is one of few vigilante true crime cases. I'll let you decide if the law ought to have been allowed to carry out justice or if Gary's act of self-appointed justice was warranted. The vast majority of American people interviewed around the time of the attack were all in favor of Gary and proclaimed he shouldn't face jail for his shooting of Jeff. There was one person who was incredibly angry and upset at Gary, though: his 10-year-old son, Jody.

Jeff Doucet's life prior to his arrest is relatively unknown. We do know he was born in Texas in 1959, although there's no information on his parents, relatives, or his upbringing. Jeff did say he was abused as a boy and that this molestation eventually caused him to go on and abuse other children while he was still a boy. As we know, the abused can sometimes go on to be the abuser, as seems to be the case for Jeff Doucet.

As he grew up, Jeff became interested in karate and would train to become an instructor. Naturally, a karate instructor's main clientele is children and young people, so perhaps it was more than a love for the sport that lured Jeff to this career choice. He moved to Baton Rouge, Louisiana, in his early 20s and got a job as an instructor, living in the same school he taught his students. It's a frightening thought that such a predator was able to freely mingle with young children at will. He was a sheep in wolf's clothing and managed to pull the wool over everybody's eyes, including the parents of his students.

In 1983, 24-year-old Jeff would be introduced to the Plauché family. He gave little Jody Plauché karate lessons and found himself getting close to his family. Jeff had no family nor significant other, so the Plauché clan gave the man friendship, even having dinner with him on one occasion. They allowed Jeff to take their son to the movies or the skate park on weekends. This worked well since June and Gary Plauché were going through a rocky patch, and Jody's outings with Jeff were thought to be helping take the boy's mind off his home life.

How wrong they were.

Jeff was using these jaunts to groom Jody. He began testing the boundaries, as Jody would later recollect, and seeing how far he could push his inappropriateness with the boy. On the way to the cinema or driving to the skate park, Jeff's hand would find itself on Jody's lap. The boy didn't feel like he could say anything. Jeff would put the feelers out by acknowledging where his hand was and insisting, "I didn't realize my hand was there," to the child. When he saw that Jody didn't run away or tell anyone, this gave the predator the confidence to gradually test the boundaries further.

When they were stretching in preparation for a karate session, Jeff's hands would again find themselves in places they should never have been. When helping Jody stretch his legs, the predator would "accidentally" grab the boy's private areas. The cautious but continuous testing eventually led to more serious assaults on Jody. The boy kept quiet for a year, fearful of the consequences of speaking up.

Since Jeff had wormed his way into the Plauché family's list of trusted people, he was free to come and pick Jody up whenever he liked. On February 14, 1984, that's just what Jeff did, except he had no intention of taking the child to the arcades or the movies. You could argue that he never had the intention of doing these things - his motive was always perversion, not kind-heartedness. This time, though, Jeff didn't bother keeping up his ruse by taking the boy on an outing. He kidnapped the now 11-year-old.

After collecting Jody, Jeff got them bus tickets to California and booked them into a hotel room once they'd arrived. The child was in grave danger, and Jeff had managed to get a head start on anyone coming to look for Jody. Plus, the Plauché family trusted Jeff, so they would presume he was simply a little late in dropping the boy off at home after a few hours passed. The twisted man used this time to his advantage and carried out the worst sexual assaults he'd inflicted on Jody.

As well as raping him, Jeff also dyed Jody's blonde hair jet black. He was passing the child off as his own in order to get away with his sick desires.

It's unclear what Jeff's plans were after his stint at the hotel with Jody. He didn't exactly have the funds to run away and start a new life - he'd been surviving by writing bad checks for quite some time. This was beginning to catch up with him, which perhaps sparked his kidnapping of Jody and running off to a new state.

Jody was concerned about his mother being worried about him. He expressed his upset about being away from his family to his captor, so Jeff let the boy call his mom. June received a collect call from an Anaheim motel and was beyond relieved to know her son was okay. By now, the FBI was involved in the case and traced the call right back to the motel. Authorities made their way to rescue the child.

Jody was rescued, and Jeff was detained, although the police were yet to discover the twisted depths of the crimes Jeff had committed.

By this point, Jody had the courage to confide in officers about the abuse that he'd been subjected to, not only in the motel but also for the previous year. Everything that Jeff Doucet had done to the boy was now out there for the world to know - including Gary and June Plauché. The parents took the sickening news hard. As you can imagine, waves of anger and frustration washed over them. They also felt like they'd failed to protect their boy, and Gary, in particular, felt overwhelmed with helplessness.

After two weeks of abuse at the hands of someone who ought to have taken care of him, Jody was finally free to go home to Louisiana.

His parents did their best to support the child after his ordeal. Gary, though, couldn't let go of the intense anger he felt. This is a feeling plenty of us can likely sympathize with; how do you deal with the vast amounts of anger and rage you feel toward your child's abuser and rapist? To know that they are breathing the same air as you would certainly be a maddening thought, particularly in the midst of finding out the extent of the abuse Jody endured.

Weeks passed by, and Gary ruminated on how to handle the situation. He wanted to avenge his boy. The only thing in his way was, ironically, the judicial system. Jeff was locked up in California. There was no way the father could get to him.

Until Gary heard that Jeff was due to be flown back to Louisiana for his trial. This was due to take place on March 16, almost a month from the date he kidnapped Jody. Quickly, Gary formed a plan in his head, and nothing would be able to stop him from carrying it out. He told no one of his plans before embarking on his quest for revenge.

Armed with a .38 revolver tucked into his boot, Gary made his way to Baton Rouge Metropolitan Airport and waited. He pulled a cap over his face and hung around. Gary was getting antsy and used a payphone to call a friend. He confessed what he was about to do. Rolling cameras surrounded the area, all waiting to get a shot of the child abuser being escorted from the plane. News stations and journalists from the local paper were readying themselves to shout questions at Jeff, hoping he would give them a quote to use in their write-ups.

"Here he comes - you're about to hear a shot," Gary warned his friend on the other end of the phone. He hung up and made his way over to Jeff, who was surrounded by an entourage and shot him once in the head. The shooting was caught on camera. As he was shot at short range, Jeff quickly froze and then fell to the floor in a heap. The cameras also caught Gary being tackled against the wall and arrested. "If somebody did it to your kid, you'd do it, too," the father cried.

Jeff Doucet was taken to the hospital to treat his severe head injury, but he succumbed to it the following day. Gary Plauché was now looking at murder charges, although nobody the press interviewed agreed with any charges being brought against the man.

Jody found the ordeal difficult to deal with. He found it tough to process that his father had done something as permanent as murder. The young boy knew Jeff was facing a long time in jail for his crimes, which was enough for him. He didn't want him dead, even though he'd done unforgivable things to him.

The people of Baton Rouge were vocal about their support of Gary. Many of them said they'd do the same thing in his situation. People who witnessed the murder at the airport agreed the man should never spend a day in jail for his act of vengeance. Gary Plauché' spent that weekend in jail. This would be the only stint behind bars he would do.

His sentence was five years probation, a seven-year jail sentence that was suspended, and 300 hours of community service. Although Gary still had his freedom, he didn't have the trust of his little boy anymore. Jody couldn't comprehend his father's actions and pushed him away. It took years for the boy to invite his father back into his life. Jody came to realize that, although he disagreed with his father's choice to end another man's life, he could acknowledge that Gary had only done so because Jeff was a bad person. Plus, he couldn't punish his father forever.

Gary completed his community service in 1989, and even as the years passed, he insisted he didn't regret killing his son's abuser and that he'd do it all over again. Three weeks before his 69th birthday, Gary passed away after suffering a stroke.

Jody, now in his 50s, has gone on to write a book about his experience and is an advocate for those subjected to sexual abuse. He attends colleges to speak to students about sexual violence and educate them on risk reduction.

What are your thoughts on this case - was Gary a cold-blooded killer or a man who felt so helpless he had no other option but to end his son's attacker's life? Cases like this often divide opinions, with people feeling strongly about their belief on what is right or wrong. No matter how you feel about the way justice was delivered, the one thing we can agree on is that Jeff Doucet was a monster.

Genie

In this true crime story, there's no murder or unsolved mystery. Still, it's one of the most heartbreaking and unfair tales I've come across. As I've said before, cases involving children hit especially hard, but this one really impacted me when I learned about it. Not only was a child subjected to unimaginable abuse, but she was also let down by the people who were later sent to protect her.

True crime cases rarely have a happy ending; as true crime followers, we already know this when we digest this type of content. However, there's something especially tragic about the story of Genie - the name given to her by authorities - since there could have been a happy ending for her, but she was let down multiple times.

For the first 13 years of her life, little Genie suffered inconceivable abuse at the hands of her violent father. Her mother is someone you could describe as weak, though some may argue the fact that fear kept her in an abusive relationship with Genie's father.

Genie's mother, Irene, suffered an injury to her head when she was just a child, giving her lifelong vision problems. This is something Genie's father used to his advantage since the woman's vision was only going to get worse as time went by, rendering her dependent on him.

Genie's dad, Clark, had a tough upbringing. He was placed into care, though he did have regular contact with his mother, who ran a brothel. It's been suggested that the boy had anger issues due to his tumultuous childhood, and these same issues are what provoked his unthinkable abuse of little Genie.

Certainly, the man knew he didn't want children. He found them an annoyance and too noisy to bear. Still, this didn't stop him from getting Genie's mother pregnant on multiple occasions. After the pair wed, it took them around five years for the woman to first become pregnant, though this didn't prevent the father-to-be from beating his vulnerable wife. In fact, his abuse of her escalated after the pregnancy revelation, and he even tried to strangle her to death on one occasion. You don't need me to tell you the negative effects domestic abuse can have on an unborn child, so it was a miracle the little girl was born at all.

I say miracle, but her short life wasn't one filled with love and adoration. Just ten weeks after she was brought into the world, her father was so enraged by her crying that he placed her in the freezing cold garage. She died of pneumonia. Their next child, a little boy, died at just two days old. Three years later, they had another son, John, who survived. He still had to endure his father's intolerance of noise and lack of care for him, though, and the boy was reprimanded for any childlike behavior he exhibited.

Clark's mother noticed her grandson wasn't being treated with much care and took him in for a short time. However, she handed him back to his parents after a few months, during which the little boy's development improved considerably. Naturally, when John was sent back to Clark and Irene, the mistreatment resumed.

Five years later, in 1957, little Genie was born in Arcadia, California. By this point, Clark's temper and maltreatment of his family had reached an all-time high. When he found out his daughter had a congenital hip problem that caused her to require a splint, he became even more disinterested in her than he already was. He believed her hip issues somehow correlated to her having mental problems, which wasn't true. The child, at this point, was developmentally fine. Even if Genie had developmental struggles, this shouldn't have been met with disgust. Instead, the child should have been loved and nurtured, two things she never got to experience.

After learning of his daughter's hip issue, Clark ordered his wife and son not to engage with Genie. Neither Irene nor little John felt they could defy the abusive man, and so Genie was often just left alone.

When Genie was almost two, her grandmother - Clark's mother - was killed by a speeding driver. The death of a parent is undeniably world-shattering, but Clark took his mother's death far worse than expected. Add to the fact that his mother was taking care of John when she was run over, Clark's disdain for his children reached boiling point. He went as far as blaming his son for his mother's death. If she wasn't out walking with the child, she'd not have been killed, he reasoned. Fueled by rage and misguided blame, Clark's abuse escalated.

He quit his job and moved the family into his mother's home, creating shrines to his late parent and further isolating his wife and children from the outside world.

Clark made the back bedroom Genie's room, although it wasn't a happy room filled with light or any form of comfort. Instead, it consisted of just a child's toilet, to which Genie was strapped for the majority of the day. The parents had made a harness that ensured she sat upright on the toilet, only able to move her arms and legs slightly. Sometimes, she was left on this contraption overnight. To be stuck on this horrific homemade device for 13 hours a day is tortuous enough - to be strapped in for days is beyond comprehension.

Her sleeping arrangements were just as dire. While she had a crib, when she was placed in it, she was zipped inside a sleeping bag. The crib would then be covered with a piece of metal.

Clark's treatment of his daughter was not only cruel and violent, it was unhinged. He was propelled by a weak wife who stood by as he beat little Genie with wooden planks for speaking. It's not like she knew words or sentences - she never did manage to learn how to speak properly - but naturally, she would try to vocalize how she was feeling. Eventually, Genie learned not to cry for help or make any kind of noise. Not only did help never come but any noise made by her was met with violence. Her father even kept a plank of wood in her room, especially for beating her with.

The little girl wasn't fed properly, either. Clark, sure enough, managed to feed himself well enough, but the child was malnourished. He fed the girl the bare minimum in order for her to stay alive, mostly baby food and baby rice. He would force the spoon into his child's mouth quickly, causing her to cough and splutter. His response to his little girl choking was to smear the baby food over her face. Genie's mother would do her best to make up for her baby's lack of food by sneaking into her room late at night and offering the child some sustenance.

Clark would often growl at his child like a dog, bearing his teeth like he had rabies, scratching her face if she cried. Because of this, Genie became fearful of animals, particularly cats and dogs.

You may be thinking that Clark was living with an undiagnosed mental illness. This would help explain his extreme lack of tolerance of noise and violent reactions to it. However, the more I learn about Clark, the more I'm led to believe he was just an incredibly bad, evil man. He had issues, for sure, but so do many of us, and we certainly wouldn't dare even think of leading a life of cruelty like he did. Evidence suggests he was of sound mind while carrying out his treacherous bouts of violence toward his family; for example, he would write down episodes of abuse and how he concealed this from outsiders.

While I've mentioned Genie's mother was weak and allowed the abuse to persist, I must emphasize just how sadistic and menacing her husband was. Not only had he isolated her from her family, he forbade her from leaving the house, and she had no life outside of her husband. Some people would say she ought to have fled to the police in the middle of the night with Genie in tow, to which part of me agrees. The other part tends to be more compassionate toward her circumstances. Irene was registered blind. She had no support, no friends or family to help drag her from the dire situation she was in. She was also much younger than Clark, who seemed to use his wife's naivety and trusting nature to his advantage. Add to the fact that Irene had no money and nowhere to go - a position Clark put her in - and then you've created a weak, dependent woman.

Clark's tolerance for any kind of noise only seemed to get worse. They had to get rid of TVs, radios, and any other noise-emitting devices from the house. Even talking was mostly forbidden. Should Irene or John converse, Clark would beat them mercilessly. The only time John was allowed to leave the family home was for school. Upon the child's return from school, he had to prove his identity before entering the property. After all, should an intruder walk in, they'd be shot. Clark would often sit with a shotgun in his lap for no other reason than to remind his family they should fear him.

Irene must have known she was her children's only hope of getting away from their abuser. From time to time, she'd ask to make a call to her parents, requests that would be met with violence from Clark. As John got older, Clark perhaps realized that the boy could summon help if he got brave enough. The cruel man made sure his child feared him far too much to speak to outsiders about his home life. He also began making John partake in the abuse of Genie, further cementing the boy's inability to seek help.

UNBELIEVABLE CRIMES VOLUME EIGHT

Clark had told his wife that Genie wouldn't live past the age of 12. He made Irene a promise that should the girl make it to 12, he'd let the woman seek help to take care of her. As you'd expect from someone as malignant as Clark, his promises didn't hold much substance. Genie turned 12, and the abuse only escalated, carrying on for another year and a half.

Then, something miraculous happened. Somehow, someway, Irene mustered up the strength she needed to stand up to Clark. Again, she'd asked to call her parents, and again, she was met with a beating for daring to request such a thing. This time, though, Irene managed to make it out of the family home - a prison by this point - and took Genie to her parents. It was late October 1970, and after almost 14 years of abuse for Genie (and even more for Irene), the pair were free.

But was it too late for Genie? Had too much damage been done? After all, the girl was practically non-verbal due to the neglect and abuse she suffered. She'd known nothing but the room she was confined to for most of the day. She'd never played with toys - she was given some wooden spoons to play with, though I can't possibly compare those to toys. Almost everything we take for granted was brand new to her.

By this point, Genie's brother had turned 18 and ran away from home. Clark was all alone in his mother's old house. He finally got the silence he'd been demanding all those years. You may suggest it would've given him time to think about his treatment towards his family and how it led to the position he found himself in: old, alone, sitting in his blacked-out living room with nothing but his shotgun for company.

Irene needed money, and she'd never claimed benefits before despite being eligible. Three weeks after fleeing her abuser, she decided to take Genie with her to Temple City and apply for disability. Next door to the disability officers was the social services building, which Irene accidentally entered on account of her being almost blind. This is an ironic yet pivotal part of this story since the woman who spoke to Irene noticed Genie. *Finally, somebody noticed Genie.*

The social worker guessed that Genie was around six and that she was autistic. To her shock, Irene told her that her child was almost 14 and had never been diagnosed with anything. The police were called, and Clark and Irene were both arrested.

Genie was admitted to the hospital while her parents were questioned as to why their child was non-verbal, malnourished, unsocialized, and showed clear signs of mistreatment. The press caught wind of the story by mid-December 1970, and the bizarre tale caused much interest from journalists and the public alike.

As such, one of Clark's biggest annoyances - noise - became a constant outside of his house. He was constantly being asked questions or to give a comment about what he did to Genie, which he never did. On November 20, Clark was due to be in court to face child abuse charges. That very morning, he killed himself. He left a suicide note that stated the "world will never understand." In the note, he didn't offer any explanation for his abuse of Genie. He also left a note to John, whom he'd also abused, to tell him he loved him.

Irene was left facing child abuse charges, although charges against her were dropped when the court heard about the severe beatings she endured at the hands of her husband. The near-blind woman had been dependent on her husband and was deemed a victim, too, and received counseling.

There was much interest in Genie from a medical standpoint, although it was uncertain if she'd survive into adulthood. She was and had been almost her whole life, malnourished. Her skin hadn't seen sunlight and was a pale, sickly color. She'd developed two sets of adult teeth. She was so used to the small room she'd been kept in that she didn't register anything that was more than three meters away from her. Her eyes worked fine; she just wouldn't look that far. The straps from her constraints had caused deep calluses.

The girl's posture was weak. She was unable to stand up straight or stretch her limbs out properly. Her walk was more of a hop. Her fine motor skills were the same as a two-year-old. She was incontinent.

Genie's stay in the hospital was not only meant to get her better physically but to help her mentally, too. The prognosis was poor - the teenager was difficult to engage with and shied away from people. She spat and drooled and would blow her nose on any fabric that took her fancy.

She was silent the majority of the time unless she had a fit of rage, during which she would attack herself. Still, she didn't scream or cry. For the most part, her facial expression wouldn't change either.

In early 1971, the linguistic team that was tasked with helping Genie figured she only knew a handful of words, one of which was her own name. Her vocabulary was just as limited, and the words she knew how to express were heartbreaking: "no more" and "stop it." By the age of almost 14, Genie had still not acquired a language. This exposes just how severe her neglect was.

Professors and scientists who spent time with Genie were divided on her diagnoses. The girl had no brain damage or other explanations for her behavior. One determined her to be extremely emotionally disturbed; another insisted Genie had been born that way.

However, as the years passed, Genie did make improvements. One of the researchers who spent a lot of time with Genie was Susan Curtiss, and she noted that the girl's improvements demolish the idea that Genie had been born that way. The leaps and bounds her development improved during her time in hospital care proved that. Susan surmised that Genie had been born with average intelligence, but the maltreatment and neglect she suffered affected her intelligence greatly.

Psychologist James Kent was sent to analyze Genie. One of the props he used to help her communicate verbally was a puppet. Genie found great joy in playing along with the puppet and it would eventually be a catalyst in her expressing emotion. James made it a priority to spend as much time with the teenager as possible. He noticed there were dozens of other people who'd been tasked with analyzing the girl, and he felt like there was no way Genie would learn to form emotional bonds if she was passed from psychologist to psychologist.

While working with James, Genie began to make vast improvements. She even began collecting items she deemed interesting. Some of these items were toys; others were normal day-to-day objects. Still, they were brand new to Genie, and she hoarded her stash of objects in her room. Her speech was slowly improving to the point she would try to mimic words and sounds she heard.

By this point, her mother began visiting. The pair had scarcely interacted in the 14 years Genie had been alive, and over the course of just a few months, the pair developed a bond. The girl would sit on her mother's knee on command, although it was noted that Genie looked uncomfortable when she did. She would seem relieved to be able to get away from her mother's embrace, likely due to the fact she'd never received affection or comfort before.

Over time, this discomfort about physical affection lessened, and Genie even began giving out hugs of her own accord to hospital staff.

In the spring of 1971, neuroscientists began carrying out brain exams on the teenager. It would be the start of numerous scans and brain tests Genie would be put through, with the aim of answering the question, do humans have a critical period for learning language?

And had that period passed for Genie?

In May of 1971, David Rigler was tasked with leading a team of scientists to study the girl. They'd acquired a three-year grant from the National Institute of Mental Health to continuously study Genie's psychological development. It was around this time she was given the pseudonym Genie.

The following month, Genie's rehabilitation teacher was granted permission to take the girl out of the hospital on daily outings. Jean Butler would take the teen to her home in Country Club Park, an affluent area of Los Angeles. Still, hospital staff were wary of Jean and her motives for her interest in Genie. However, Jean was doing what nobody else had done: socializing the girl outside the confines of her hospital room. Eventually, Jean applied to be Genie's foster carer. While a decision was to be made, the teen was permitted to stay with her rehab teacher. Physically and mentally, she flourished in just a few short months with Jean, who was childless and single.

She worked with and observed the girl, even managing to show her how to use the toilet successfully. Genie's incontinence had all but disappeared. As time passed, Jean began to resent the number of people who were tasked with poking, prodding, and testing Genie and began to push back on sessions with researchers. Jean was doing her best to look out for the girl, but this frustrated researchers who felt the woman was holding the girl's development back.

Eventually, Jean's application to be Genie's sole carer was denied. When Genie was told she'd not be staying with Jean any longer, she cried out, "No, no, no." While Jean may have hindered research on Genie, there's no doubt the girl felt comfort and care while living with her. It seemed as though what Genie wanted was never a consideration.

The teen was then placed in the care of David Rigler, a therapist and psychology professor. He and his wife, Marilyn, took Genie in until a permanent home could be found. They guessed they'd have her for a few months, but the couple took care of the girl for almost four years.

During this time, she met with her mother for lunch once a week. The Riglers certainly didn't want Genie to cease all contact with her mother, but they remained acutely aware that Genie was only in this position, in some part, because of her mother. In fact, many of the scientists and researchers who dealt with Genie found it hard to hide their dislike of the woman due to her inaction in seeking help for Genie.

Meanwhile, Jean Butler began voicing her concerns that Genie was being put through harmful tests against her will and that the grant money was not being spent correctly.

Still, the girl was showing signs of social improvement. Before, she would simply walk away while someone was talking to her; now, she began to engage when people were interacting with her. She'd hold eye contact well. She would even begin taking interest in conversations going on around her, even ones she wasn't part of, much like a precocious child.

Her social skills had advanced so much that she managed to attend a nursery for underdeveloped children. She still had a lot to learn, though, and taking things that didn't belong to her was one of Genie's vices. Still, she began to react with a sense of guilt upon being caught for taking others' belongings, signaling she knew it was wrong to do so.

By mid-1975, the teen had improved but was still exhibiting the effects of under-socialization and abuse. Still, if you pointed toward an object, much of the time, she could name it. Cup, plate, pen, and bed were all words she hadn't known just a few short years prior. However, while she could name items, she still couldn't place these words in a full sentence. Her vocabulary was short, and her conversational skills were limited. This helped scientists realize that knowing words and being able to use them in conversation were two separate skills to learn altogether. The latter was proving to be incredibly difficult for Genie.

It was concluded that Genie had failed to learn language during the critical period of her childhood and, as such, would likely never have a full grasp of any language. However, the snippets of conversational ability she had were often telling. "Father is angry," she was heard saying, along with "Father hit." She said these things to no one in particular, suggesting that not only did Genie remember the abuse, but she carried it with her.

The researchers began to ask her questions about her past, and she managed to convey that her dad would beat her, spit at her, and make her cry.

However, the National Institute of Mental Health began questioning what they could learn from Genie. No solid scientific data had been collated from researching Genie. The plethora of teams analyzing Genie all had muddled data. The funding for her was pulled.

By now, it was 1975, and Genie had turned 18. She went to live with her mother, who struggled to take care of the young woman. I say she was a young woman, but she had the mind of a child, and this was something Irene wasn't prepared for. The mother quickly contacted the California Department of Health to seek out a different home for Genie. This led to her being bounced from foster home to foster home, many of whom physically and emotionally abused her.

The vulnerable young woman soon regressed. She began wetting herself, her incontinence resurfaced, and her conversational ability all but disappeared. In one disgusting incident, Genie vomited and was violently attacked for doing so. As such, she refused to open her mouth in case she was sick again, further making her more withdrawn and insular.

After noticing the severe setbacks this foster home was causing Genie, she was removed from their "care" in 1977. After a fortnight in the hospital, she seemed to come round and be open to short conversations. Still, she was sent to yet another foster home, and the constant moves took their toll on Genie. She didn't know why she was being passed around and began to believe it was her own fault that no one would offer her a permanent home. Again, she reverted to not vocalizing and avoiding interactions.

Right up until the early 90s, Genie was passed from home to home. Researchers who managed to keep in touch with her noticed she was depressed and insular. Since interest in the woman declined, little is known about what happened to Genie or how she improved as she got older.

It was reported in 2016 that she was a ward of the state of California and living in a private facility. Her mother died in 2003, and her older brother passed away in 2011. He'd not had much contact with Genie at all since her escape from her abusive father.

If Genie is still alive today, she will be in her late 60s.

The torrent of abuse and torture Clark inflicted on his child was something she had to battle with her entire life, and no doubt still battles with today if she's still alive. In his suicide note, he stated that nobody would understand. He was right, although his lack of explanation perhaps shows there was nothing to understand. He was simply a cruel, twisted man who knew his actions were abhorrent yet never did anything about it. And, because of that, a child suffered in ways none of us will be able to comprehend.

Pyromaniac

The term pyromaniac refers to someone who is unable to resist starting fires. The fire starter gets gratification from lighting fires and watching them burn. However, fire is often uncontrollable and thus deadly, and many pyromaniacs end up killing to get their kicks. The tale of Bruce George Peter Lee (born Peter Dinsdale) is one such story. He managed to kill 26 people over a six-year spree of arson attacks.

Born in Manchester, England, in 1960, Bruce (then named Peter) didn't have a stable upbringing. His mother was a sex worker, and the boy was brought up in the care system. He never met his father, who ended his relationship with Bruce's mother while she was pregnant. The boy was bullied growing up due to his congenital disabilities in his right limbs, with other kids mercilessly mocking his arm and calling him cruel names.

On the list of Bruce's bullies was his own mother. She mocked him for his disabilities, letting the boy know he was a disappointment to her. Naturally, the boy grew up with an unhealthy sense of self, knowing only bullying and loneliness.

Due to the bullying and being placed in schools that only catered to the physically disabled, Bruce didn't flourish academically. In fact, his education was almost nonexistent.

As he made his way into his teens, Bruce began working, taking on manual labor jobs to help him get by. When he was 19, his mother got married, and the teen was invited to live with her and his stepfather. In doing so, he changed his surname to that of his stepdad, which was Lee. He also changed his first name from Peter to Bruce, in homage to his favorite martial arts star.

For years, Bruce had been dealing with urges to start fires. According to him, his fingers would begin to tingle when he got the urge to set something alight and watch it burn. The only way to get rid of the "tingles" was to start a fire, something Bruce discovered when he set fire to his local mall. Over £17,000 worth of damage was caused by the teenager. Bear in mind, this occurred in the mid-70s, so £17,000 equates to well over £100,000 now.

Still, the boy got away with the crime since it was ruled accidental.

Bruce got the fire-starting tingles regularly and didn't fail to act upon them. However, the fires were ruled to be an accident each time, and the teenager evaded justice time and time again.

Another time the teen let his fire-starting urges get the better of him was when he had an altercation with an older man about some pigeons. In 1973, when Bruce was just 13 years old, he set alight 34-year-old David Brewer after the man had hit the boy for bothering his pet birds.

As David sat sleeping on his sofa, Bruce crept into the man's property and set him alight. David awoke, engulfed in flames, and screamed for help. Neighbors arrived and flung soaking wet towels on the badly burned man's body.

Sadly, David wouldn't survive this attack. His death was concluded to be accidental since it was thought he'd hung clothing too close to his open fire, and this was what caused the fatal incident. Never in their darkest thoughts could law enforcement think a teenage boy had done this out of malicious revenge.

The teen struck again the following year when he killed 82-year-old Elizabeth Rokahr. The frail older woman struggled to get about, and her eyesight was failing, so when the teen set her living room alight, she didn't stand a chance at getting out. As he watched the flames engulf her little terraced home, the pensioner burned alive. Yet again, the death was ruled an accident. Elizabeth had been a smoker, and it was determined that she'd fallen asleep with a cigarette in hand, unwittingly causing the blaze and killing herself.

In the summer of 1976, the sadistic teen would claim another life - a one-year-old boy named Andrew Edwards. On this fateful night, he was being taken care of by his grandmother, who was babysitting his older siblings as well. The woman managed to get little Andrew off to sleep and placed him in his crib in his upstairs bedroom. However, the woman was alarmed to discover a fire blazing from her upstairs cupboard, and in her panic, she ushered her two eldest grandchildren from the home. With the children in tow, the grandmother alerted a neighbor, who called the fire brigade.

The fire was spreading rapidly, and all the woman could do was stand outside and watch helplessly as it ravaged her home. In her flustered state, she'd completely forgotten about baby

Andrew - until the fire brigade arrived and asked the horrified gran if there was anyone inside the building. The sickening realization hit her that Andrew was in the blaze, but by this point, there was no way for her to run back inside the building. As you can imagine, the grandmother was distraught and blamed herself for her grandson's death.

Once the fire had been put out, an inquest occurred to decide the cause. Again, no foul play was suspected, and it was decided that Andrew - the one-year-old - had started the fire. It was determined he must have found some matches and lit them. I'm sure stranger things have happened, but this most certainly wasn't the case. The inaccuracies of the findings only served to make the grandmother even more blameful toward herself for the fire, resulting in her being committed to a mental health hospital. The trauma of what she'd seen and the belief that she'd let it happen drove the woman to madness.

In reality, the fire had been started by 16-year-old serial fire starter Bruce George Peter Lee. He would go on to commit dozens more murders. He would read about the lives his attacks took in the papers the day after they took place, but this wasn't enough to make him turn himself in. He would later claim those who died due to his fire-starting impulses weren't intentional murders, but it's hard to believe that when he ended up murdering dozens of people. I can't think of any other person in history who has killed dozens of people "accidentally" by repeating the same act over and over again.

At the beginning of 1977, Bruce struck again, this time killing a six-month-old girl named Katrina Thacker. Bruce knew the Thacker family but became disgruntled when they reprimanded him for walking into their home uninvited. Unable to deal with this perceived "rejection," the almost 17-year-old decided to do what he did best - set them on fire. While it seems he may have tried to target the entire Thacker clan, when he snuck in and set the living room alight, his only victim was the baby girl.

Mere days later, he'd strike again, adding even more victims to his macabre tally. The boy had access to a residential home called Wensley Lodge, which was home to a large number of older men.

On January 5, 1977, the night care worker on duty was doing his rounds when he saw smoke emanating from the first floor. Immediately, he raced to a co-worker and told them to ring the fire department. Although it didn't take long for firefighters to arrive, the fire spread quickly. The raging flames took the lives of Harold Akester, Victor Consitt, Benjamin Phillips, Arthur Ellwood, William Hoult, William Carter, Percy Sanderson, John Riby, William Beales, Leonard Dennett, and Arthur Hardy. These eleven men, all pensioners, all vulnerable, and all looking to live their twilight years in comfort, were cruelly killed at the hands of a pyromaniac whose lust for fire was only getting stronger.

As well as the men who died, the fire also caused a number of injuries to residents who were lucky enough to survive the quickly spreading flames.

Just like the previous arson attacks, it was ruled an accident. By happenstance, the same day Bruce set the home alight, a plumber had been working in the very room the teenager had started the fire in. His work required the use of a blowtorch, and as such, the fire was considered to have been triggered by this. Yet again, Bruce had gotten away with his wicked crime through pure luck.

A few months later, in the spring, he took the lives of two more children, seven-year-old Mark Jordan and 13-year-old Deborah Hooper.

The Hooper family had invited a friend to stay, and the friend brought his sons, one of whom was Mark. After socializing that night, the family went to bed, with Mark's dad sleeping on the sofa. In the early hours, the man was awoken by a fire. He raced upstairs to tell his friend, who was fast asleep in bed with his wife. The adults rounded up the children, and the fire showed no signs of relenting. By the time they'd made it outside, they realized that they only had two of the kids with them.

Deborah hadn't made it out, so little Mark had raced back in for her. The considerate child hadn't been able to understand the danger he was confronted with, and both children died in the fire. Posthumously, Mark received a bravery award for his courageous and thoughtful act that took his life.

Again, Bruce wasn't captured for his crime. The man who fell asleep in the living room had not only lost a son but was blamed for falling asleep smoking a cigarette, thus causing the fire. He had to live with the (untrue) knowledge that he'd ended the life of his child and a teenage girl.

The following year, in January 1978, the 17-year-old struck again. He killed almost an entire family after setting their terraced house alight. Mother Christine Dickson, 24, and her four children, all aged under five, were engulfed in the flames, dying an unimaginable death. Her husband and father of the children managed to flee through the front door, but the mother died trying to save her babies. Christine had managed to pass one baby from the burning house before succumbing to the flames, and that child would be taken care of by its grandmother. Yet again, the blame for the fire was placed on the children of the house, with an inquest believing the two eldest boys had been playing with matches.

They hadn't been; a teenager with twisted impulses was ravaging the local area with his fire-starting, but nobody was suspecting foul play. As such, Bruce was free to give in to his urges as soon as they struck him. Each time, his desire to light fires was taking lives, ruining families, and causing destruction. This didn't faze the teenager much. It was collateral damage.

The next winter, Bruce killed again. Charles Hastie, 15, Paul Hastie, 12, and Peter Hastie, aged eight, were all victims of his latest bout of pyromania. On December 4, 1979, Bruce made his way to the Hastie household, where the brothers and their mother lived. The siblings (plus their other brother, Thomas) were fast asleep, as was Edith Hastie. They awoke to find their home ravaged by fire.

The eldest, Charles, thought fast and saved his mother by forcing her to the upstairs window and pushing her out. The fearful mother was hesitant to leave her kids inside, but Charles made sure to push his mother to safety, whether she was willing to or not.

By this point, though, the flames had taken over every exit possible for the boys. The scorching flames not only prevented them from escaping but also quickly engulfed the young boys. They were sadly burnt to death. It is a sickening way to die as an accident, but a truly cruel, evil way to die when the fire is started purposefully.

Thomas was the only Hastie boy who made it out after firefighters made their way to the back bedroom and found the fire hadn't managed to do as much damage there.

By a stroke of luck, the three Hastie sisters - Angeleena, Nicola, and Sophie - were all sleeping elsewhere the night of the fire. The patriarch of the family had been doing a stint in jail at the time the blaze occurred but was released on compassionate grounds after finding out three of his boys had died horrifically.

Amazingly, this fire wasn't deemed an accident, nor was it blamed on the kids. Immediately, police noticed paraffin at the front door, which, unbeknown to everyone, was Bruce's preferred ignition. Authorities knew this was no accident, so to get a bigger picture of the situation, they created an incident room in the local church. Here, they would invite local people in to talk about the tragic accident and the Hastie family. To the police's surprise, people weren't too bothered about the fire. The death of the boys hadn't had much of an impact on the community at all, it seemed. This was unusual, especially when you consider the agonizing way the boys' lives ended.

The apathy from the locals didn't go unnoticed, especially by Edith, who broke down at her boy's funeral and scolded the community for their indifference to her kid's death.

After speaking with locals, the police figured out the Hastie boys were disliked by the community, having been viewed as a problematic group due to their penchant for violence and crimes. It seemed the trio had made plenty of enemies in their short lives, and the police believed the attack to be one carried out in revenge.

One of the locals who willingly attended the incident room was Bruce, who admitted he knew the Hastie boys. As well as Bruce, the police spoke to dozens of other teens who knew the Hasties, but law enforcement kept coming back to Bruce as a line of inquiry. Eventually, six months into the investigation, to the shock of everyone, the young man made a full confession.

Not only did Bruce confess to starting the fire, he said he did so because he'd been in a sexual relationship with Charles, the eldest boy. However, Charles was only 15, and Bruce was almost 20. This made the "relationship" illegal. Charles, according to Bruce, began extorting money from him for his silence. If Bruce didn't hand over the cash, Charles threatened to tell the police about their entanglement. So, Bruce did what he did best and set the Hastie house alight in revenge.

However, Bruce had more to tell the police. He confessed to nine other fires, all of which had been considered accidental, over the past six or seven years. The police were skeptical of this claim, believing the boy might have simply been looking for attention. Plus, there was no reason for him to have set fire to the residential home or any other of the properties he claimed to have burnt down. He had no grudges or vendettas here. So, the police took the young man on a ride around all of the locations he claimed to have committed arson and, subsequently, murder. To their surprise, Bruce recalled the precise place in each location where he'd started the fire. Only the police knew this information. It seemed Bruce was telling the truth, making him a killer of over two dozen people.

Still, officers were slightly dubious about his story. On the off-chance that Bruce was just a fantasist who somehow managed to acquire police intel about the fires, they accused him of starting a fire they knew he didn't commit. In fact, they already had the culprit for that particular fire. They simply wanted to test his honesty. Bruce denied all involvement in that fire, insisting he had no involvement and knew nothing of the fire. It seemed Bruce wasn't a fantasist as first believed.

One question, aside from why, remained. Was Bruce sorry for the multitude of deaths he'd caused? No, he said. Murder wasn't his intention, he claimed, although I struggle to digest how murder wasn't intentional when he targeted homes and buildings he knew were full of people. Residential homes, shopping malls, and family homes late at night all tend to be pretty full of people. Fire kills people with unflinching ease. How he could claim his murderous rampage was unintentional is something I find hard to comprehend.

In October 1980, Bruce was charged with 26 murders alongside a plethora of other crimes, including causing grievous bodily harm and arson. Plenty of his crimes had caused life-changing burns and injuries, but the victims luckily survived. Bruce would deny murder but put in a plea of manslaughter. This was accepted since he wasn't considered of sound mind when he committed his crimes, and he was sent to a psychiatric hospital.

Three years later, another inquiry was conducted on the residential home fire. Surprisingly, it was determined that Bruce couldn't have been responsible for it, thus quashing his manslaughter convictions for this case. Despite the findings, Bruce still accepts responsibility for the fire.

Bruce married a fellow patient from his psychiatric hospital in 2005. It's been suggested that the criminal, now in his 60s, may never be released.

The Witch

Pop star, witch, and... cold-blooded killer? It's not often you hear those three descriptions in the same sentence. For the case I'm about to cover, though, that sentence is entirely accurate.

Maznah Ismail was born in January 1956 in Malaysia. She was a natural entertainer from a young age, singing and dancing for her family, who encouraged her to pursue her talents as a career. In her teens, she began using the stage name Mona Fandey, and it was under this name she released her first album in 1987. She was a mild success in her native country, although she never truly reached stardom.

She had a few TV bookings here and there, but the limelight she sought after seemed to be out of reach. Later on, she would certainly have the spotlight cast on her, but definitely not for her singing talents. She married and had a daughter, all the while pursuing stardom. However, the marriage wouldn't last, and the divorce was finalized in the late 70s.

She went on to marry a man named Mohamad shortly after, who essentially became her manager. He not only helped her book gigs but also funded her career. However, it became clear after a few years that the singing sensation Mona wanted to be would likely never materialize. The woman needed to find a way to make an income. She practiced witchcraft and went on to become a witch doctor, two practices she would monetize.

This career proved far more fruitful than her dreams of stardom. Her clients steadily got more high-profile, to the point she was servicing politicians. After all, during election periods, these people needed as much power on their side as possible. They sought out Mona for her skills in magic and witchcraft, hoping her spells would quash their competition.

Word spread among wealthy communities of Mona and her supernatural abilities, and the clients kept rolling in. As such, so did the money. The woman became rich from her client base, owning top-of-the-range cars, dining in five-star establishments, and buying up any mansion that took her fancy. She lived a life so many of us dream of, with money being of no concern and luxury at every turn.

In the summer of 1993, Mona was approached by Datuk Mazlan Idris, a politician who was intent on becoming the Head of Government of Pahang. But, in order to do so, he needed some supernatural help to give his career a push in the right direction. He made it clear to Mona that he wanted to be at the top of his political party's ladder, and she'd been recommended by a number of his political friends whose careers were flourishing. Mona agreed to take Datuk on as a client and promised him success in his career.

The witch told her new client that she'd need to perform a ritual with him in order to turn his aspirations into reality. She told Datuk to lie on the floor and close his eyes. His partaking in this ritual was crucial for the spell to work, so the man did exactly as he was told. Mona then told her customer to picture money raining from the sky above him, and as the man was imagining a bountiful of notes falling onto him from the clouds above, something did actually fall onto him. It was a sharp ax to his neck.

The blade sliced right through the man's throat, detaching his head from his neck.

Less than a day later, Mona took herself off to Kuala Lumpur to do one of her favorite things: shop. She didn't just buy clothes and beauty products, she really went to town with her splurging. Mona bought a new cell phone - a rare luxury in 1993 - brand new sofas, new cabinets for the kitchen, a top-of-the-range TV, and a video camera. Oh, and a new car and a new nose.

Meanwhile, Datuk had been reported missing. His last known movements were on July 2, when he withdrew large sums of money from various banks in Kuala Lumpur. This was in the lead-up to his planned meeting with Mona to carry out the "ritual."

On July 13, police officers arrested Mona and Mohamad's assistant, Juraimi Hassan, for unrelated drug offenses. They brought the man in for questioning, though he gave them more information than they bargained for - he confessed to killing Datuk Mazlan Idris. Not realizing the police only had drug offenses against him, he made a full confession, leading police to one of Mona's properties where the body was allegedly buried.

Sure enough, they found Datuk, though his body wasn't intact. He'd been skinned, and his limbs had been removed. In total, they'd chopped the man up into 18 pieces, burying his remains in a deep hole covered with cement. Mona's home felt ominous, even before officers discovered the human remains. The woman and her husband kept axes and knives as ornaments, and they had an altar installed on their property.

Mona, Mohamad, and Juraimi were all arrested for murder.

It turns out that Juraimi was the one to land the fateful blow on Datuk at his employer's request. It's not known why the victim was skinned, but it may have been part of a more sinister ritual that Mona and her cohort carried out after the killing.

The three were tried in 1995, and the murder caused a media frenzy. Not only because the case involved voodoo and witchcraft, things that were revered in Malaysia at the time, but also because one of the accused used to be a semi-famous pop star. Ironically, Mona generated more buzz and fame from her involvement in a gruesome murder than her singing and dancing ever did. Though, she didn't seem too bothered by this. In fact, the 30-something appeared to be basking in her newfound stardom. Fame and fortune had been all she'd ever wanted. She'd acquired the latter in abundance, and now she'd finally attained the former.

Newspapers and journalists had a field day as the trial took place. Mona would arrive at court in expensive attire, dressed to impress. She didn't bow her head in shame or try to hide from the flashing cameras as she entered court - she'd smile and pose for the baying crowd of reporters. Instead of the editorial spreads she'd dreamed of getting as a young girl, she was getting front-page headlines for being a murderer. Still, it seemed that to Mona, any publicity was good publicity.

The trial lasted just over two months. Juraimi took the stand and turned on his former employers, though he admitted his part in the killing of Datuk. He confessed he had beheaded the man but only did so under duress from Mohamad. His employer also commanded him to chop the man up before burying him.

As Juraimi told it, Mona and Mohamad brought the victim home and got him changed into a sarong. Once he was in proper ritual attire, the pair then led Datuk to the bathroom, where they laid him down and told him to close his eyes and imagine money falling from the sky. As she asked him to think of the cash raining on him, Mona draped an orchid on the man's face. Once the victim was in a peaceful, docile state, Mohamad ordered Juraimi to chop his head off, a command he followed.

Afterward, according to Juraimi, the husband and wife took a shower together to rid themselves of the blood that had sprayed on them.

Mohamad's version of events is a little less believable. He claimed that he and his wife were carrying out the ritual as planned, bathing their client in flowers, when Juraimi burst into the bathroom with an ax in hand. Unprovoked and without reason, the man then chopped Datuk's head off.

Mohamad claimed he and his wife ran off in fear, though his trauma at the event prevented him from reporting the murder to the police.

Still, despite being so (allegedly) traumatized, Mohamad managed to find the strength and clarity to forge Datuk's signature and transfer the victim's wealth and land over to himself.

Mona, the main attraction in what was becoming a circus of a trial, refused to be cross-examined. She did offer the courtroom a handwritten statement whereby she categorically denied all involvement in the murder of Datuk Idris. The shopping spree she carried out mere hours after allegedly watching Datuk's murder didn't help the jury believe her statement.

Mohamad also said that Datuk owed him a large sum of money for a talisman he'd sold him. Perhaps this could have been the truth, although we'll never know, but it may have been another motive in the murder.

With Juraimi turning on his former employers and giving evidence against them, the couple was found guilty of murder and sentenced to death. Despite Juraimi working with the police, he, too, was found guilty and was given a death sentence. His counsel appealed this since Juraimi had been considered to be vulnerable due to his low intelligence. The appeal was declined.

When Mona was informed that she would be hanged, her reaction wasn't one of shock, fear, or panic. Instead, she smiled and gave a big thank you to "all Malaysians." Her exit from the court was photographed as usual, with her smiling and posing for the reporters who waited for her.

Naturally, with someone being so cool, calm, and collected after committing a murder - the woman went on an all-expenses-paid shopping trip - you have to wonder if she'd done it before. This is a question the Malaysian police asked themselves, too.

When the murder of Datuk came to light, law enforcement started to look a bit deeper into Mona's history. Sure enough, no less than five of her housemaids had suddenly disappeared over the years.

Mona had acquired something of a cult following over the years and had an abundance of rich and powerful people who swore by her witchcraft. One of them was a man named Tan, who admired Mona for her talents and was once a high-paying client of hers. Tan also brought in his wife for Mona to work her magic on.

In the summer of 1993, their decomposed bodies, along with their baby son, were found at two different burial sites. The family had been reported missing years prior, but nothing had ever come of it. Their bodies, just like Datuk's, had been mutilated and cut up before being buried. Mohamad, through happenstance or guilt, also owned the land where the dismembered bodies were found.

The police delved deeper into the theory that Tan and his family were victims of Mona and her bloody voodoo. They spoke to his sister, who gave them an interesting story. In the lead-up to their disappearance, Tan's wife made a frantic visit to her sister-in-law's home, begging for a lump sum of money. There was no explanation as to why she needed the money nor why there was such an urgency for it.

Police surmised that, since the woman visited without her five-month-old baby, the child had been kidnapped for ransom. The anxious visit was made in order to obtain the funds to pay the kidnappers, which the woman managed to collect in time to get her baby back. Except, she didn't get her baby back. The kidnappers - alleged to be Mona and Mohamad - killed the family in order to stop them from going to the police.

Malaysian police also connected Mona to the murder of a woman named Irma. In 1992, her body was found in various locations and had the same modus operandi as both the Datuk and Tan killings. However, when her dismembered body was initially found, there were no leads or lines of inquiry to follow. It was only after the macabre discoveries of other bodies that the police put two and two together.

Other evidence also surfaced to tie Mona to Irma's murder. When police officers searched her property after digging up Datuk's body, they found a sickening discovery - jars of organs. The internal organs were found to be human and are believed to belong to Irma.

Despite the strong evidence to suggest Mona and Mohamad had something to do with these murders, they were never tried for them. Perhaps officials thought there would be no point since the pair were going to die anyway.

The husband and wife, along with Juraimi, were all on death row until November 2001.

In the lead-up to their hangings, Mona and Mohamad spent the day with their family, having been allowed to spend eight hours with them before they met their maker. It was reported, as you can imagine, that plenty of hugging and crying took place, with Mona's daughter and Mohamad's sons saying their last goodbyes.

Amidst the tears, Mona said something interesting: that she would never die. It could be that she believed in something higher, or maybe she believed her witchcraft had rendered her immortal. Maybe she had created a spell whereby she would be reincarnated - nobody knows what she meant by this since she didn't elaborate.

The hanging was set for the dawn of November 2, 2001. The trio declined a last meal and simply wanted to get the ordeal over with. The criminals had hoods placed over their faces, and their wrists were cuffed. The gallows had been prepared in advance with three nooses hanging from the sturdy beam above. After they were led to the trap, their legs were tied together, and a thick rope was placed around their necks. Just before 6 am, the trap doors collapsed, and the three bodies dropped down with a sharp tug on the rope.

Hangman

Killer cops could be a true crime category all on its own. For some reason, crooked cops or police officers with dark secrets seem to be a more prevalent theme in crime cases as of late. Is that because we have less of a tolerance for dishonorable behavior from those who ought to protect us? Or is it because of the rise of the internet and social media, whereby information and incriminating evidence can be shared within seconds? Or, has the public awareness of police corruption just not been there in prior decades?

Whatever the reason for the revolt, it's still a disturbing thought that a handful of those who promised to serve and protect did the complete opposite of those oaths. One of these cases took place in 1970s Florida.

The tale begins in March 1946 in Wisconsin, when Gerard John Schaefer was born to Gerard and Doris Schaefer. Gerard Senior was a traveling salesman, so the family moved frequently but eventually settled in Florida when Gerard Junior was 14.

The boy didn't get along with his father well at all. In fact, Gerard would accuse his dad of being abusive, a drunk, and an adulterer. Gerard Senior's treatment of his daughter was, in stark contrast, loving and full of adoration. Naturally, this upset the young boy, who found comfort in his mother.

In school, Gerard was somewhat of a loner, though this was because he chose to be, not because he was cast out by his peers. He did have friends but wouldn't place himself as part of a group, preferring to spend his free time alone in the forest. To his classmates, he was considered "outdoorsy" and someone who simply liked being in nature instead of around people.

But, as the boy grew older, he began dealing with sexual urges that centered around him hurting himself. Eventually, the desire to inflict pain on himself developed into his wanting to hurt women in a sexual way.

While exploring these new, violent fantasies, Gerard began wearing women's underwear. He'd take himself out to the woods, tie himself to a tree, and find ways to inflict pain on himself. He was just 12 years old when he began this behavior, and it was only going to escalate.

Though, if you look back at Gerard's earlier childhood, you can see it started much earlier, albeit to a lesser extent. In playing games with his sister, he'd ask to be the character who was hurt and killed. He'd also play the feminine role whenever they played make-believe games. As a young boy, although he didn't realize it, Gerard enjoyed the idea of females dying a horrible death.

As the boy grew into his mid-teens, he developed a reputation for being somewhat of a creep among his female classmates. So much so that if a girl wore a skirt that day, she knew to tuck it tightly behind her when Gerard was about. The teen wasn't covert in his tendency to look up his classmates' skirts, causing young females in his class to be wary of him.

Despite his less-than-charming reputation among his peers, Gerard was a good student and did well academically. He was known to be a gifted sportsman and was part of the football team, though again, he didn't make many genuine friendships during his time on the team.

Gerard enrolled at Broward Community College, majoring in social studies. His grades would drop here, but he still managed to get a scholarship to Florida Atlantic University. His goal was to be a teacher, hoping he could encourage his students to have "American values," including "honesty and purity." While at university, Gerard became concerned about his increasingly violent thoughts and his inner voice telling him to kill. He sought therapy, which didn't help, and the young man subsequently continued to fantasize about harming women in unimaginable ways.

In 1968, he married the young woman he'd been dating named Martha. The marriage didn't last two years, with Martha filing for divorce in early 1980. Her reason for wanting out of the union was vague, but knowing what we know now of Gerard, it was believable: she said he was extremely cruel.

By this point, Gerard's dreams of becoming a teacher had been all but demolished. He'd managed to get a couple of teaching internships, but his lack of knowledge on the subjects he taught - namely geography - would hinder his progress. It wasn't this that ended up getting him fired, though - it was complaints from students' parents. Gerard had been very vocal about his moral and political beliefs and tried his best to indoctrinate his students with these firmly held beliefs. Initially, his employers tried to give the young man guidance on his teaching style and warned him off trying to mold the pupils in such an intense way. Gerard's refusal to heed this advice saw him being sacked.

After his divorce, Gerard spent some time in Europe and, upon his return, was ready to reassess his career. His teaching aspirations went nowhere, so he decided to pursue another career he'd always been interested in: law enforcement. He placed a number of applications to various Sheriff's offices, in which he lied about being fired, instead completely fabricating his role and experience at the school he previously worked for. Most police departments passed on Gerard's application, except a small division called Wilton Manors.

Shortly after his welcome into the police force, Gerard was commended for his role in a police raid, but any high praise for him quickly waned. He simply wasn't a good police officer; he was seen as lazy and ineffective. His behavior while on duty also became troublesome. His chief found out that Gerard had been pulling over vehicles driven by females and running their license numbers into the police database. This enabled the sneaky man to find out their home addresses. Once he let the women drive off, he'd note down their personal details and turn up at their homes randomly, asking them out on dates.

This is disturbing behavior, no doubt. The fact that Gerard had remarried recently didn't seem to faze him or make him think twice about this behavior, either. When he was eventually caught for his perverted scheme, he was fired. He managed to secure employment quickly after this, surprisingly as a police officer at Martin County Sheriff's Department. There was no way he could use his prior boss as a reference - after all, he remarked that Gerard didn't have "an ounce of common sense," not to mention his immoral work ethic. So, in order to secure the Martin County role, he falsified a letter of recommendation from his old chief.

You would imagine that Gerard might take this opportunity to straighten up, appreciate the job he'd been entrusted to do, and begin abiding by the oath to not betray public trust. Gerard did none of these things.

Less than a month into his new role, he was up to his old tricks. Only, this time, he wanted to ramp up the danger element.

It was a scorching day in July 1972, and two young hitchhikers were thumbing their way to Stuart, Florida. Nancy Trotter, aged 18, and her friend, Paula Wells, aged 17, were shocked to be confronted by a police officer telling them that hitchhiking was illegal in Martin County. The girls were sure it most certainly *was* legal, and they were right. But who were they to argue with the officer advising them of the law? The teenagers accepted they'd broken the law and hopped in the policeman's car, who told them he'd drop them off in Stuart.

The officer on duty was Gerard Schaefer, and he did as he'd promised; he drove the girls to their destination and dropped them off. On the way there, the girls talked about where they'd been and their plans for their trip, one of which was to visit Jensen Beach. Before parting ways, Gerard told the teens that he could pick them up the following day and get them safely to the beach - he didn't want them getting arrested for hitchhiking, after all.

Thankful to the helpful officer, Nancy and Paula gratefully accepted the gesture and agreed to be taxied to the beach just after nine the following morning.

You may think the girls were naive to accept a lift from a stranger like this, but it's important to remember that Gerard was not only in full police officer uniform, the girls heard him talking on the radio, they'd seen his name badge, and he had all the accessories a police officer would need. There was no doubt in their minds that this man was a genuine policeman, and again, they were right. However, just because he wore the uniform didn't mean he was free of bad intentions.

The next morning rolled around, and the girls met up with Gerard in the agreed place, but they were shocked to find he had casual clothes on and his police car wasn't anywhere to be seen. He had an explanation for this, though; he was undercover that day. His car had to be unmarked to keep up the ruse. The man was convincing enough to get the girls in the backseat, and off they drove to Jensen Beach.

Gerard would make the teenagers feel uneasy this time, though. He began warning the girls of the dangers of accepting lifts from strangers, explaining the slavery market was looking for two females just like them.

Eventually, Gerard pulled up at Hutchinson Island, insisting to his passengers that there was interesting stuff there. He mentioned there was some old Spanish architecture to see, and he was happy to walk them there. The girls weren't in too much of a position to argue or demand anything from the increasingly inappropriate man. They would simply thank him for the lift and make their own way to their desired destination. Sadly, they didn't get a chance.

As the trio were walking through the forest, Gerard attacked both girls, cuffing and gagging his terrified victims. After binding both girls, he tied them to separate trees a short distance away from one another. He tied their legs with rope and put a noose around their necks, forcing them to use their feet to balance on the tree trunk underneath them. The girls knew murder was imminent; Gerard explicitly told them he was going to kill them. After raping them first, he added. Plus, their attacker had given away his real name - it had been on his police badge. They knew they wouldn't be getting out of this ordeal alive.

Then, by sheer luck, Gerard's radio went off. He was required immediately at the station. He had to put his torture killing on hold and told his victims he'd be back. He also goaded them about trying to escape, warning them he wasn't going far, so he'd find them anyway. The man hopped in his car and left the two girls hanging.

The police job took Gerard around two hours to complete. He returned to the forest to resume his abuse of the teenagers he'd bound to the trees, only to be shocked to find they weren't there. Panic set in; he knew the girls would head straight to the police and give them his name. So, trying to exercise some damage control, Gerard rang his Sheriff and told him he'd done something stupid. He also warned Sheriff Robert Crowder that he may be mad at him before explaining how he tied two teenage girls to a tree in the forest.

That was the extent of the truth he told, though. He didn't mention he was going to rape and kill his victims. Instead, he said he was "teaching them a lesson" for hitchhiking and getting in cars with strangers. He told his boss he just wanted to scare them from being so risky and trusting. However, Gerard admitted to the Sheriff that he may have gone too far in his chastising of the girls.

Meanwhile, a truck driver had found Paula running through the forest in a terrible state. Police officers were alerted and sent to check the wooded areas, where they found a soaking wet, bound girl with her clothing shredded. She could barely talk but told them her name and that her friend was somewhere in the woods, too. Officers told the distressed young woman that her friend was safe and at the police station, much to Nancy's relief.

Both girls not only identified their attacker, but they also gave the police his full name. As well as being fired with immediate effect, Gerard was arrested for assault and false imprisonment. His bail was set at $15,000, which he paid 10% of in order to be released. He was back in the streets shortly after his initial arrest.

It's a troubling fact that, had the former police officer been refused bail, he wouldn't have been able to carry out any more attacks. Sadly, the twisted man made the most of his freedom to carry out his deviant desires.

His trial for the attack on Nancy and Paula took place toward the end of 1972 when he pleaded guilty to assault, but all other charges were dropped. The former police officer got a year in jail and three years probation. His sentence began mid-January 1973.

However, what Gerard had gotten up to during his time on the streets was beyond what anyone thought he was capable of. The September prior to his trial, he abducted two more girls. They wouldn't be so lucky as to escape his clutches.

Susan Place, aged 17, and Georgia Jessup, aged 16, were attending the same adult education center as Gerard. He introduced himself as "Gerry Shepherd" and got talking to the girls. He feigned interest in their likes and interests, agreeing with their taste in music and their beliefs in reincarnation. In reality, the man was simply trying to gain their trust, which he did successfully. The girls, in their youthful naivety, considered him a friend.

When "Gerry" suggested they take off together, the girls agreed.

Susan's mother came home one day to find an older man hanging out with Susan and Georgia. He assured the concerned mother that he only had good intentions for the girls, and Susan said they were all going to the beach and would play guitar there.

Still, Susan's mother, Lucille, felt uneasy about this older man spending time with her daughter and her friend. While she didn't stop her child from leaving with the man, she made a note of his license plate.

When Susan said goodbye to Lucille, the parent noticed her child was teary-eyed. Something felt off - like the girl was leaving home for good. Still, Susan promised her mother she would only be gone briefly but would keep in touch. Whatever "Gerry" had told the teen, it had prompted her to want to run away with him. Georgia would take off from her family home, too.

A day passed, then two, then three. Susan hadn't gotten in touch. Lucille was beyond anxious and felt regret about letting her daughter walk out the door. She wanted Susan to be independent and didn't place many restrictions on her, but in this instance, she wished she'd followed her gut instinct to forbid her child from leaving home with an older man. By day four, the overwhelming worry caused Lucille to call Georgia's mother to see if she'd heard from Susan. To Lucille's shock, she learned that Georgia had left home and not returned as well. The mothers quickly reported their children missing, and Lucille made sure to hand over the license plate number that belonged to "Gerry."

It was quickly established the plate didn't belong to a "Gerry," nor did it belong to the green car it was attached to. The person whose plates had been stolen looked nothing like the description of Gerry that Lucille gave to the police. The police had no leads, and the girls were simply labeled as runaways, which wasn't uncommon for the time. The case went cold. Little did Lucille know, the police had noted the license plate number she gave them incorrectly, so they'd had the right information all along but didn't make use of it properly to trace the man.

Months passed, and Lucille figured she'd have to do her own digging, which she did in the spring of 1973 when she found a letter from Gerry in her daughter's room. Written on the letter was a return address that she drove to in Stuart, Florida. When she got to the building, she spoke with the property manager, who confirmed the real identity of the man living there: Gerard Schaefer. The building manager also divulged a lot more, telling the mother how the criminal wasn't home because he was doing jail time for trying to hang two young girls in the woods. Lucille's stomach was in knots. She asked when Gerard was sent to prison. "January this year," the manager told her. Her daughter went missing the prior September when Gerard was very much on the loose. She asked for a description of Gerard, and sure enough, it fit the man she saw drive off with her daughter.

Lucille went back to the police and told them about the discovery and also got them to double-check the license plate number she gave them. Sure enough, they'd gotten it wrong. When the real number was put through the system, it led them straight back to Gerard Schaefer's vehicle. The inmate was brought in for questioning over the disappearance of the two girls, but he denied any knowledge of Susan and rejected Lucille's story of having spoken to him the day her daughter left home. When the police department showed Lucille Gerard's mugshot, she matched him straight away to the man who drove off with her daughter the September prior.

Still, there wasn't much the police could do. There were no bodies, no evidence, and nothing concrete to tie Gerard to the crime.

The following month, a man was collecting cans on Hutchinson Island when he happened upon a sickening discovery: the decomposing bodies of two girls. The remains were sent to the forensic pathologist, and four days later, the bodies had been identified. Using their dental records, the bodies were confirmed to be Susan Place and Georgia Jessup.

Analysis of the young women and their plethora of injuries - they were described as being "butchered" - matched the modus operandi of Gerard's other confirmed attack. It was apparent the girls had been tied to the tree they'd been buried near. Their heads had been chopped off, their jaws had been shattered, and they bore the injuries of a machete attack. Susan's jaw had a bullet hole in it.

The sick murder had all the markings of an attack that Gerard would carry out - the tree torture, the ripping of the clothes, and the procurement of two young girls to enact his twisted fantasies on. Not to mention, Lucille had pinpointed him as the last person her daughter was seen with.

A few days after the discovery. Gerard's family home was searched, and his bedroom provided an excess of evidence against him. When his old chief proclaimed Gerard hadn't "an ounce of common sense," it seems he was accurate in his analysis of the criminal.

Inside the man's room were heaps of women's jewelry, hundreds of pages of crude and disturbing stories written by him, and drawings of depraved acts being carried out on women. The stories he wrote, sometimes typed, would all have a similar theme: young women, often teenagers, being hung after their rape. In these tales, there were paragraphs upon paragraphs of how the victims would be humiliated before their eventual hanging.

The disturbing stories would often not end after the victims had been killed. Gerard continued writing, explaining how the protagonist - himself - would return to the burial site of his victims and abuse the corpses. It was clear from his thousands of words worth of writing that Gerard had a macabre enjoyment in women wetting themselves out of fear. The writings also depicted Gerard returning to the decomposing bodies of his victims to pull their teeth from their now-exposed skulls.

The more officers found the more they had to ask: was this sick collection of stories not, in actual fact, just stories? Were they true accounts of the sick acts Gerard Schaefer had carried out over the years?

The more evidence they found, the more the latter seemed to be the truth.

Gerard had bags upon bags of guns, knives, and rope mixed with pictures of himself with a noose around his neck, tied to a tree. In one of these pictures, he was in women's underwear and had excrement smeared on him. Even more disturbing were pictures of possible victims: women with horrific wounds, mutilated beyond recognition. The backdrop of these pictures was believed to be an hour and a half away in Davie, Florida. However, the quality of the pictures caused them to be insufficient to put forward as evidence.

Gerard had also been conversing with a pen pal from Australia. Disturbingly, it seems during his travels as a younger man, Gerard met a kindred spirit: another man who enjoyed the same violence and depravity that Gerard did. In their letters, this was clear to see. The pen pal enclosed images of women who had been fatally mutilated, females who had been disemboweled, and other women who had been brutally attacked with machetes.

Among the piles of upsetting material was a jewelry box. There was indeed jewelry inside - one item belonging to a woman named Leigh since that was the name engraved on it - but there were also other items, such as teeth. It was ascertained from the loose teeth in the box that these had been removed from eight separate victims.

There was also another incriminating find - the IDs of Barbara Wilcox and Collette Goodenough, two young women who'd been reported missing at the start of 1973. They vanished one week before Gerard was sent to jail. The teenagers' skeletal remains would later be found in 1977, though their bodies would be so decomposed no cause of death could be determined. As a result, no charges were filed against Gerard.

Then, there was a stack of newspaper clippings the man had collected. One such clipping referred to the 1969 vanishing of Carmen Hallock. Among Gerard's twisted hoard was Carmen's gold-filled tooth. This, again, wouldn't be pursued as the evidence wasn't strong enough to stand up in court.

As time went by, more personal belongings were being linked to their owners. In every instance, the person whose jewelry was found was also missing. The jewelry of 14-year-old Mary Briscolina and 13-year-old Elsie Farmer was found in his stash a year after their disappearance. Once their bodies were found, again, their decomposed state rendered their cause of death impossible to find. Yet again, another case crumbled due to lack of evidence, though law enforcement knew who the culprit was. They just couldn't prove it beyond reasonable doubt.

With all the evidence collated from his mother's house, Gerard was looking like one of the worst serial killers in history, racking up dozens of victims over a short span of time. As the victim list kept getting names added to it, but no tangible evidence was found to secure a murder conviction, investigators decided to just charge the man with the murders of Susan and Georgia. He was convicted in late 1973.

Gerard, unabashed, would appeal 20 times at this sentence. The man was unlikely ever to get out, but he scuppered his chances at any kind of parole when he admitted many more murders in letters to his like-minded friends. In them, he laughed at how the police had asked for confessions, but they were already there in the stories he'd written; the police were just unable to see that.

He also estimated his kill list to be between 80 - 110 victims, spanning almost a decade of murder. He also spent time in Europe and various other places after university and in between jobs, something he alluded to when he noted his crimes crossed "three continents."

Then, he began musing as to what actually counts as a "kill." If he slaughtered a pregnant woman, would that be classed as double murder? What about those who died of shock as they watched their friends being mutilated before them? Or what about the woman who choked on her own vomit? Was that his fault, too? The despicable man penned these rhetorical questions in a way that sounded more like gloating than it did a genuine question.

The letters expose Gereard as unrelenting and utterly detestable. It seems his fellow inmates also found him loathsome, as over the years, they subjected him to various acts of malice. His cell was set on fire multiple times, and on various occasions, other prisoners would throw their human waste at him. There was certainly no fan club for the killer, and he was often suspected of being an informant, which he was.

One of Gerard's enemies - Vincent Rivera, a killer from Tampa - burst into his cell on December 3, 1995, with the intent of doing him some serious harm. With a knife in hand, he stabbed Gerard over forty times in the head and face area, piercing his eyes and totally removing his right eye. The violent attack was fatal. Gerard Schaefer was 49 years old.

When learning about his death, the judge who handed him his life sentence remarked that Gerard had finally gotten the death sentence he deserved. Georgia Jessup's mother proclaimed she wanted to send Vincent Rivera a gift for finally getting justice for her daughter.

While he was only convicted of two killings, the police have found evidence for at least two dozen more. If Gerard's ominous stories and letters are true, though, he could be one of the world's most prolific and sadistic killers ever to have existed.

The Hike

Jolee Callan was 18 years old and excited for the life she had ahead of her. She was just about to start college, she had a trusted circle of friends, and the teen had an undeniable lust for life. She was known to dye her hair frequently, often choosing bright pinks and purples, which tied in with her bright and outgoing personality. The popular girl had just endured a break-up, although it perhaps came as more of a relief than it did a heartbreak to her.

Loren Daniel Bunner, her former boyfriend, had been controlling and possessive of Jolee. He didn't like her spending time with her friends and tried to make it so the only person she spent time with was him. He was allowed a social life, though, so should he meet his friends, Jolee would be brought along. Sometimes, Loren's treatment of Jolee would frighten or upset her into breaking it off, but every time she did, her boyfriend would threaten to end his own life if she left him.

This is typical narcissistic, manipulative behavior used to control and coerce. For a short time, Jolee was unable to see this. However, after ten months together, the teenager sensed her increasingly possessive boyfriend was only going to get worse in his treatment of her, so she broke it off for good. Any threats Loren made of harming himself weren't met with the reaction he wanted.

After ending the relationship with Loren, it didn't take the bubbly teen long to meet someone new and begin dating again. It was clear the girl valued not only her independence but understood her worth, an understanding many of us don't acquire until well past our youth.

Still, Jolee didn't like to upset anybody, much less make enemies. So, she kept in contact with her former flame. Plus, they'd bought a dog together, and with Jolee having a soft spot for animals, she wanted to be given updates about the pet. The teenager was very clear to Loren about their relationship status, though - they were just friends. When he texted her on August 29, 2015, asking to go on a hike, she agreed. They hadn't seen each other for a while leading up to this invite. It would be one last hiking trip, she said, a symbolic way to ease them out of a romantic relationship and into a strictly friends-only basis.

After agreeing to the walk with her ex, Jolee texted her friend to let her know she'd agreed to meet Loren as an act of closure for them both. "If something happens to me, you know who I was with, " she joked to her friend. As the saying goes, there's a speck of truth in every joke.

The following day, Jolee and her family dog, Kiba, headed out to meet Loren, and the three made their way to the picturesque Alabama countryside. They embarked on the Pinhoti Trail in Cheaha State Park, a seemingly happy and fun-filled walk that was documented by Loren's multiple posts on social media. The images he uploaded were of the scenery and of Jolee taking in the breathtaking views.

Little did Jolee know Loren had more than just water and snacks in his backpack. He'd also brought a .22 Bear Claw with him, and his intentions for the hike certainly didn't involve closure or friendship.

The very last photo of Jolee is her on the cliffside, taken by Loren. With her back to him, Loren pulled out his gun and shot the teenager in the back of the head. She didn't fall off the cliff as he presumably expected but fell to a heap on the floor. The twisted attacker then walked over and turned Jolee onto her back, where he shot her again right between her eyes.

Nothing had happened prior to Loren shooting her. There was no argument, no upset or crying over the failed relationship, and there was no tension. Still, after shooting his ex-girlfriend, Loren rolled her off the 40-foot cliff, ensuring she'd not make it out of his sick attack alive.

Afterward, Loren walked back to his car, blood spattered all over him, and called the police. He admitted he'd killed Jolee Callan and told law enforcement exactly where they'd find the body. As the police made their way to the scene, Loren sat in his parked car, awaiting imminent arrest. However, he hadn't been able to tell the 911 call handler the full story: that he and Jolee had a suicide pact. They'd headed to Cheaha State Park that day to carry out their plan. But, after killing his ex, Loren discovered he wasn't able to turn the gun on himself.

When he was eventually apprehended by the police, he managed to tell them this. Perhaps it was clear to them at the time, but this was just a weak fabrication from Loren to get him off the hook for murder.

The trial began around three months later, in November. Loren was doubling down on the notion that he and Jolee had both planned to end their lives that day, and they'd arranged to leave this world together. When it came to Loren keeping his end of the bargain, he sobbed that he couldn't do it.

Evidence from Jolee's family painted a different picture of the teen. They said she'd been making plans for the future and was excited at the opportunities in front of her. There was no way, they said, that Jolee would kill herself. She'd never want to leave her family or friends, nor would she want to do it with Loren. He had been a source of anxiety for the teen, and when they finally managed to get out of the relationship, it hadn't been painful for the girl. Rather, she felt relief.

The prosecution told a story of a jilted lover driven by jealousy and anger and said Loren had planned out Jolee's murder because she refused to be his girlfriend. Loren had hoped the hike would force the girl to change her mind about getting back together, and when it didn't, he took his gun out and ended the teenager's life. All because, through his own controlling actions, she chose not to be in a romantic relationship with him. It's a story that has sadly been repeated throughout history.

Loren's defense argued that the killer had Asperger's syndrome. To me, I don't see this as any kind of defense. I know people who have Asperger's, and I can honestly say none of their symptoms have ever been close to plotting murder, let alone carrying one out. It could have explained, to some degree, Loren's difficulty in processing and dealing with the emotions of the breakup.

But, if you look at the bigger picture, the teen was known to be controlling, coercive, and manipulative toward his girlfriend prior to killing her. This would explain the excessive anger and rage he felt when she eventually left him, not Asperger's syndrome. His ego had been dented, his control had slipped, and his ability to manipulate had been taken away from him the moment she stopped giving in to his threats of self-harm.

Loren's attorneys put forward that he should be given youth offender status since he was under 21. This would mean that the highest sentence he could have received for the murder was three years in prison. The request was granted.

Three years in jail for taking the life of a young woman who had the world at her feet. What would this teach the criminal about consequences? How much "reformative" work could you do with the killer in just three years? Could you truly trust someone who'd killed someone in such a cold-hearted way not to do it again?

The result caused an outcry. So much so Loren had to wear a bulletproof vest upon leaving court. The public was so outraged that it was feared someone might try to take justice into their own hands.

Jolee's father spearheaded a petition to have the youth offender status removed from Loren. It was an insult to Jolee and an insult to proper justice. Michael Callan tallied to have the decision overturned, requesting that Loren be tried as an adult and face the full force of the judicial system. The heartbroken father spoke to his local TV station and was vocal in the media about his upset at the ruling.

The frenzy and outrage, both from the Callan family and the local community, caused officials to haul Loren back to court and annul the initial youth offender status he was given. He was re-trialed in the summer of 2017, where he pleaded guilty to killing Jolee. His defense team did try to reduce his sentence by claiming he was mentally ill, though they didn't provide enough evidence of this to sway the decision: 52 years in jail.

Loren must serve at least 15 years before he can apply for parole.

Mother

Gretchen and William Crooks lived in a rural home in Osage, Iowa. Together, they had a 13-year-old son called Noah. Life was picture-perfect, and they were a happy family with a home filled with love.

To imagine a member of the Crooks family was capable of murder was laughable. Even more unbelievable would be the idea that teenage Noah would be the violent culprit.

Gretchen, 37, was a nurse at Mercy Medical Center and was well-known to be a hard worker who never shied away from going the extra mile for her patients. She was known to be kind and always had a smile on her face, even after a long, difficult shift. She was in the process of getting a master's in nursing administration, further cementing everyone's suspicions that nursing was Gretchen's life. In short, as well as being a loving wife and mother, she was beloved in the workplace, too.

On the evening of March 24, 2012, Osage Police Department call handler Barb Michael received a call that she'll remember forever. "I just shot my mom," the youthful voice said. While prank calls weren't uncommon, they usually weren't as twisted as this. Barb listened intently, and she quickly realized the young boy on the other end of the line was serious. "I'm not joking," he said.

He confessed to Barb that he was scared, admitting that he didn't know why he did it, but he shot his mother before trying to abuse her body. "I tried to rape her," he told the call handler, who was understandably shocked by this admission. It was hard to harmonize the young voice with the vile things he was confessing to. "I couldn't rape her. I tried to."

The boy was apologizing for what he'd done, telling Barb that he wished his mother would just wake up so he could hug and kiss her.

At this point, you may feel small pangs of sympathy for the distressed boy. He'd just done something so atrocious and permanent, and his young mind was realizing the enormity of his actions. But Noah's regret wasn't fueled by guilt or remorse. He told Barb as much. "I'm never going to be able to get a good job now," he moaned. "I'll have to move away." He also complained that the plan he had for himself: marrying his girlfriend and going to a good college, was ruined. "I am going to jail," Noah sighed.

The police were on the way to the Crooks, and Barb made sure to keep Noah updated on their whereabouts so the boy didn't get spooked when they arrived. Noah wondered if the police officers were going to shoot him for what he did. Barb reassured the boy that they would not.

William Crooks was out at a work social event that night, but Noah had texted his father after he'd brutally shot Gretchen.

I killed Mom accidentally. Come home now, please, the boy messaged his dad. William knew his son could have a dark sense of humor sometimes, and he also knew he could butt heads with his mother from time to time. William brushed the message off as a joke and even replied with his own, telling his son to throw Gretchen's body in the grove.

Officers knocked on the Crooks' front door, and a skinny red-headed boy answered it. He did as the police told him and sat on the porch as officers headed inside to gauge the scene. To their dismay, everything Noah had told Barb was true. Gretchen was covered in bullet holes, slumped on the sofa, and covered in blood. She'd been wearing a pajama set that evening, the top half of which was open. Her bottoms had been removed.

Let's rewind the clock back to earlier that evening. Gretchen had made her son some food, homemade donuts, while the boy was in his room. Noah was an avid video game fan, particularly shooting games. However, some recent bad grades had meant Gretchen had taken his favorite video game from him. Still, his room was filled with everything a teenage boy could want. Despite the game being temporarily taken from him, he still had more than enough to keep himself occupied. But, the punishment made him angry.

After setting the donuts out to cool, Gretchen sat on the sofa, placed her laptop on her knees, and began studying. She shouted up to her son that his food was ready, and he made his way down the stairs.

Just moments before this, unbeknown to Gretchen, her son had snuck down the stairs with a rifle in hand, ready to shoot her. However, she had been busy making his snack, so Noah didn't carry out the attack then. He didn't find it "honorable" to shoot his mother while she had her back turned to him. In other words, he wanted her to see his face when he was pumping bullets into her. And that's exactly what would happen.

Just before 7:30 pm, after being shouted down to grab his food, Noah pointed the gun at his mother. Gretchen had time to comprehend that her son had fired a bullet at her. Then he shot again and again. A total of 21 bullets pierced Gretchen's head, torso, and neck.

After killing his mother, Noah began removing her clothing and made an attempt to rape her. This proved unsuccessful.

With the crime scene cordoned off and Noah arrested, there was just one more thing to do: inform William that his son had killed Gretchen. Little did officers know Noah had already told his father this but wasn't believed. As soon as officers called the father, he raced home to be met with what must have felt like a living nightmare: his wife filled with bullet holes and his son the admitted culprit.

For anyone to do this to your wife would render you heartbroken; for it to be your own son who carried out this despicable crime, I'm not sure how you'd ever be able to process that knowledge.

Noah was charged with murder and assault with the intent to commit sexual abuse. However, he was only 13 years old. You had to be 14 years old to be tried as an adult, which is what law enforcement was angling for. If he were tried as a "youthful offender," he would receive a much lighter sentence and be back on the streets in just a few years. It was a tough case for investigators. They'd never had to deal with something so bizarre and barbaric before. Because it was new to them, they were unsure how to navigate it.

Meanwhile, Noah's maternal grandmother spoke to the press to say not only had she lost a daughter, she'd lost a grandson, too. People who'd known or worked with Gretchen were speaking out to pay tribute, and each and every person mentioned the woman's kindness, her work ethic, and her big heart.

While people were mourning and paying their respects to Gretchen, her son was sitting in a youth offender facility, waiting to hear his fate. The boy had no previous convictions, was an average student, and wasn't seen as overly problematic. Though he'd had a couple of incidents at school where he'd been placed in detention for fighting on the bus, that's about the extent of his bad behavior.

As investigators were doing their best to figure out a motive or whether Noah had mental health problems, Gretchen's funeral took place on March 30. It was noted the boy didn't express emotions and that he didn't cry. He seemed calm in the face of everything he'd done.

Eventually, his defense team had come up with their strategy: to plead insanity. Diminishing Noah's responsibility would mean less time locked up and would make it so he wouldn't need to go to prison but a mental health facility instead. The judge also determined that Noah was to be tried as a youth. Still, it was agreed that from psychological evaluations carried out on Noah, he wouldn't be ready for release by the time he was 18.

The boy had no mental health issues or psychiatric struggles. He was coherent and goal-driven, the doctor analyzing him found. Noah hadn't killed his mother in the heat of the moment or by "accident" like he told his father - he'd planned to do it and stuck to his plan. The fact that doctors had nothing to treat except a lack of conscience made rehabilitation difficult for them. There is no therapy or pill that can cure callousness, and each doctor who was asked to analyze Noah had the same opinion: they were pessimistic about treating him.

The boy's trial took place in April 2013 and opened with his defense team telling the court that Noah was suffering from IED - intermittent explosive disorder - when he killed his mother. The disorder sees the individual exhibit episodes of anger and sudden violent outbursts in which the person loses control of themselves entirely. In a nutshell, one word to describe the disorder could be "impulsive." This is what the defense suggests Noah felt when his mother took away his video game.

However, Noah wasn't impulsive. He planned and schemed. In fact, he canceled the first attempt at taking his mother's life because she was facing the wrong way. There was a quarter of an hour between the first and second attempt, so it wasn't a sudden outburst.

Noah sat and watched as his dad gave evidence. The boy looked at his lap mostly, not looking overly concerned; in fact, his expression was relatively blank. William testified that Gretchen was the one who would lay down the rules in the household, but did so from a place of love. He told the court that although mother and son could argue, they'd often make up just as fast and be sat watching TV or playing games together afterward. As a whole, William said that Noah and Gretchen's relationship was a loving one.

William was then asked if his son had ever threatened to kill Gretchen in the past. The father admitted the boy had, in fact, admitted to wanting to murder his mother. "I didn't take it as a threat at the time," William told the court. He simply thought his son was upset at his mother, and it was a comment made in dark humor.

The defense team also used some of Noah's classmates to show the boy had mental health issues. Some of them testified that the boy was violent and would stab other pupils with pencils and that he'd threaten to kill them. Ominously, classmates also admitted to hearing Noah talk of killing his mother. Those who went to school with Noah all agreed the boy was angry and easily triggered, be it by losing on his videogame or at a game of football.

The prosecution had testimonies from the doctor who assessed Noah. One doctor mentioned how Noah was mentally coherent and not suffering from any illnesses. He also mentioned that the boy could calmly explain what he did on the fateful day he murdered Gretchen without a flicker of remorse.

Another doctor agreed, stating that Noah knew right from wrong. He called 911, after all. But, she also highlighted the content of the call: most of the call for "help" was Noah complaining that his life was over, that he wouldn't get into college and his dream job aspirations were down the drain. It was all about him. He had no concern for the woman he'd just murdered and tried to defile - the same woman who'd cared for him and loved and nurtured him for 13 years.

The jury had to decide whether Noah was insane at the time of the killing or if he was a cold-hearted killer who knew exactly what he was doing. The jury deliberated for 17 hours and found Noah guilty of second-degree murder - not the charge of first-degree murder he'd been tried for. Still, this verdict meant Noah would be behind bars for potentially five decades.

Noah stayed out of trouble while incarcerated and was still made to attend school while he was given mental health treatment.

His case was looked at yearly in a bid to see how Noah should be handled moving forward. In his 2016 assessment, it was noted that Noah had refused to acknowledge why he killed his mother. Even when his father confronted him about Gretchen's murder, all Noah had to say was that he thought his father would be better off without her. The teen had years to think about what he'd done, but he still hadn't shown an ounce of regret.

It was also mentioned that Noah, by his own admission, was arrogant about the crime. The teen had thought the worst punishment he'd get was being grounded by his father.

When pressed about how he felt the day he shot his mother almost two dozen times, Noah admitted he didn't feel angry and even told his counselors that he loved his mother. They had been very close. The family as a whole, the teen said, was tight-knit. Still, he could never explain why he killed his mother. Or, rather, he never wanted to explain why he killed Gretchen.

The outcome of this assessment was the suggestion Noah be incarcerated for 45 years. The teen had offered no way for physiatrists to gauge whether or not he'd be able to be integrated back into society. The fact that he refused to delve into his heinous crime is enough to let them know it's not safe to consider releasing Noah. The sentence was welcomed by William, who told his son, "It's just what it is, kid, you need to pay for your mother's life." Despite this, William remained in contact with his son despite not getting the answers he needed from his only child.

Soulless

Cases where injustice after injustice takes place can be a heavy tale to learn about. For the victim at the center of the case, we feel endless amounts of sympathy and frustration on their behalf. There was a quote I read the other day, something along the lines of *the only time people think about injustice is when it happens to them*. I wholeheartedly disagree with that comment since I think about injustices every day, spending hours thinking how they could have been avoided and how hellish it must have been for the victim. The following true crime is one of those cases.

Grace Packer - not her birth name - was born in August 2001 to two individuals who abused her and her siblings. It was discovered that little Grace had been sexually abused and was taken into care. Her parents tried to regain custody of their children, a fight they were unsuccessful in. As a result, the baby was sent to an orphanage, where she stayed until she was three years old.

Sara and David Packer adopted little Grace and brought her home, along with Grace's younger brother, to Pennsylvania. Other families adopted the other siblings, and so the children's contact with one another was cut overnight. Still, Grace was a resilient little girl - she'd had to be. Despite her tough start in life, she was known to be a deeply caring and empathic girl, even from a young age.

The Packers had fostered dozens of children over the years and decided they wanted something more permanent. Because of their reputation as reliable fosterers, there were no concerns over the Packers bringing the two youngsters into the family. For Grace, that simply wasn't true.

While her younger sibling was treated with care, Grace was treated with contempt. Despite only being on the planet for a few short years, Grace had had barely any respite from cruel adults. Sara would hit Grace if she felt the girl had misbehaved, as well as yell and scream at her. Punishment would also include banishing the girl to her room or even locking her in the basement. This maltreatment would continue for a decade.

Grace had learning difficulties, but Sara didn't care to make allowances for this. She'd scold the girl for "not being normal" and would either treat her as a non-entity or treat her with utter malice. There was no in-between.

Then, in 2010, the Packers got a knock on the door from the police. One of the children they'd previously fostered had made some disturbing allegations against David. According to the complaint, the teenager said David would force her to wear revealing clothing and would often tie her to the bed. She also described her room as being directly opposite her foster carer's room and said David would enter whenever he pleased and force himself upon her.

In cases like this, the police can often find it hard to make an arrest. It's too frequently brushed aside as a "he said, she said" situation, and a conviction is never secured. (As an aside, I read the other day that in the USA, out of 1,000 reported rapes to police, only six result in a jail sentence: 0.6%. A sobering statistic.)

However, David had recorded the abuse on his phone, and there were pictures of the assaults that enabled the sick man to be sent to prison for his crimes - for 18 months to five years. Discussing the length of the sentence, or rather the lack of length, would mean veering away from the case. Still, I will mention that prior to being sent to prison, David admitted to sexually abusing other children, too, including Grace. He told police officers that Grace had been five years old at the time.

After David was jailed, things began to crumble for Sara, too. She had a good job in a senior role at an adoption agency, of all places, but she was subsequently fired after David's conviction. She was also banned from being a foster carer moving forward, but somehow, she was able to keep guardianship over Grace. When you discover how these types of cases end, you come back to these moments and wonder, *how was that allowed to happen*?

Sara ended her relationship with David while he was behind bars, and she met a new man named Jacob Sullivan. Years passed, and Sara took Grace wherever she went until, in the summer of 2016, she reached out to the police to report her daughter missing. By this point, Grace was 14 and had been acting out, according to her mother. When Grace wanted to visit a friend, but Sara refused to let her go, an argument ensued, causing Sara to send the teen to her room. Sara then told officers that Grace had stolen $300 before taking off.

The investigator leading the case of Grace's disappearance asked Sara for an up-to-date photo of the teen to aid them with their search. Sara agreed she'd dig one out and hand it in the next day. The mother didn't bother handing a photo to officers, nor would she answer police calls. For two months, she dodged officers, and when officers tried to pay the family home a visit, they found it was empty.

Sara's weird behavior was scrutinized, and it was discovered that she'd taken Grace and her brother out of school without explanation. Her brother was re-enrolled in a new school, but Grace wasn't.

Eventually, investigators caught up with Sara at her new property. She apologized profusely for not handing a photo in and not keeping in touch. She promised she'd give them the picture the following day, which she did.

As part of the investigation, it was also revealed that Sara had only recently begun telling family members that Grace had run off. It had been months by this point, and it seemed she'd hidden her child's sudden vanishing from them for some reason. This was something else that pricked up investigators' ears. Surely, if your child goes missing, a child with a learning disability who was vulnerable, you'd be beside yourself until you found she was safe. Sara seemed apathetic.

A public appeal for information on the teen's disappearance brought up nothing.

Then, a strange letter, apparently written by Grace, was found in her school records. In it, she apologized to her family for being a "burden." The typed letter, addressed to Sara and penned for the whole family, was a poor attempt to mimic Grace. The girl had her own way of writing and spelling certain words; the pacing and grammar didn't match Grace's, nor did it have her tone of voice. It was clear the girl didn't write this. But who did, and why?

The investigators turned to Sara, who had been collecting Grace's Social Security disability checks while her daughter was missing and was looking like a prime suspect.

In October 2016, hunters found a body in a remote area. First, a torso, then some arms and legs. Then, the head. The sickening discovery was reported to the police, who identified the body as Grace's.

Sara was suspect number one. A search of Sara's home found nothing - except one interesting receipt for a bone saw. The woman was arrested but denied murder, having no recollection of the bone saw purchase. The police were unable to find the tool anywhere on the property. Jacob posted the bail money for his partner, and Sara was free again.

Shortly thereafter, the police received a phone call from a woman who'd been in a polyamorous relationship with Sara and Jacob. The pair had overdosed in an apparent pact, and she'd found them. The plan didn't work, and when Jacob awoke in hospital, he confessed everything. He was guilty of Grace's murder. Not only that, he and Sara planned it so they could rid her from their lives while still cashing her disability checks. The man also admitted to sexually abusing Grace before killing her.

In 14 short years, everywhere Grace turned, she was used and abused, with nowhere to turn for help. Those who ought to protect her did the complete opposite.

The truth of Grace's final hours on earth came out. That July, Sara and Jacob drove the teenager to one of their rental properties. They fed her supper laced with drugs. Before she blacked out, Jacob punched the girl in the face multiple times, causing her to bleed and busting her lip wide open.

Then, with Sara's encouragement, Jacob dragged Grace to the attic and gagged her. He hog-tied the victim before carrying out a horrific violation of the girl. He raped her while Sara stood and watched. Despite never receiving compassion or love from her adoptive mother, as this attack was taking place, Grace turned to Sara and pleaded for help. The cold woman refused, telling the girl that this was "her life now."

The evil enabler then stood back to spectate the vile abuse she was orchestrating. Jacob would say that Sara seemed to relish in this role. The initial plan was to keep the girl in the attic "for Jacob." However, it is soon decided that Grace has to die. They didn't want to make it quick or painless - they wanted her to suffocate to death slowly.

They gagged her and stuffed her tiny frame into a closet in the attic. The weather was sweltering, even for July, and the couple knew the girl would struggle to breathe. The evil couple headed out for a few hours and, upon their return, went to check on the body. However, Grace hadn't died: she'd managed to free herself of the gag and bound wrists and was out of the closet. So, Jacob suffocated her himself.

The pair then dragged the corpse to the bathroom and used the bathtub to dismember her. Then, they poured cat litter over the remains to hide the smell. However, this proved to be useless, and the pair decided to put the body parts into plastic bags and bury Grace in the woods.

Jacob's confession saw them both arrested with no bond set. Jacob would plead guilty to murder. Part of his confession tapes were played in court. In it, he was laughing as he described the part where Grace looked to her mother for help. He also smirked and smiled as court proceedings took place, as did his equally contemptible partner in crime.

Sara also pleaded guilty and admitted to hating Grace. "I wanted her to go away," she said. She offered Grace to Jacob as a way to avoid losing him and tried to minimize her involvement and enjoyment of watching Grace being abused. The prosecution would state that Sara was the one who suggested and instigated the sexual abuse of the victim. Not only that, they alleged that in her relationship with David Packer, she was the one who encouraged his abuse of the children. Then, there were messages on Sara's social media where she offered a stranger a virgin to abuse. It's a maddening thought that this woman fostered at least 30 children over the course of her life.

Sara got life in jail for Grace's murder. Jacob got death, and when sentencing him, the judge told him he had no soul. Repentance or remorse didn't creep in for Sara, who laughed about Grace's death with other inmates, calling her daughter a "witch."

In the spring of 2020, aged 47, Jacob died of a heart aneurysm. Sara remains in jail, where she'll stay until she meets her maker.

Malicious Matriarch

Over the course of this series, I've covered multiple cases that surround a vulnerable, child-like victim (some of which are in this volume). You may feel the same as me when a crime is carried out on an adult who only has the mental capacity of a child; it evokes the same heart-wrenching pangs as if the victim were actually a child. This is the case for the forthcoming story, which begins with the birth of Cheri Lynne Brooks in Ohio in 1962.

The family home was filled with abuse and neglect, so at the age of three, Cheri and her three siblings were placed into foster care. While Cheri spent years in the system, she eventually returned to her mother when she turned 16. By this point, her mother was single and welcomed her child back into her home.

Upon reconnecting, Cheri told her mother that she'd had a baby while in foster care but that authorities were withholding the baby from her. This incensed the mother, who did her best to provoke Cheri into pursuing custody of her child. In the end, though, Cheri had to tell her mother that she'd lied: there was no baby.

This senseless lie would be one of the thousands Cheri would tell over the years, having picked up a habitual lying habit, perhaps for attention.

After leaving foster care, Cheri would spend much of her time with her biological family, including the extended family members, of which there were many. In particular, she spent a lot of time with her cousin, Daniel Bixler. After a short while, the pair would cross the line and embark on an affair, although the family eventually learned about it. This wasn't met with anything but acceptance, even when they had a child together, a little boy called Scottie.

In 1981, the boy was removed from Cheri's care after some disturbing allegations about her abusing the boy came to light. She was accused of sexual abuse.

Over the next few years, her relationship with Daniel fizzled out, and she married a man named Mike Maloney. The pair had a son together in 1983, whom they named Josh. However, social services soon became aware of the situation and began to monitor the family. It became clear that Cheri wasn't able to meet her baby boy's needs, often giving him cow milk since formula cost too much. Cows milk, though, can be dangerous for babies, a fact that Cheri knew.

The young mother refused any support offered to her. She was eligible for help that would provide her with food and diapers for her baby, but she wouldn't take it. As such, little Josh suffered. The lack of nutrition and the stream of cow's milk he was fed only served to cause him stomach pains. The boy ended up with colic, causing the baby to cry at the top of his lungs due to the discomfort.

As you may know, there's nothing you can do to soothe a baby with colic. No amount of cuddles, rocking, or winding will quiet their crying. All you can do is comfort them until it passes, though this isn't something Cheri and Mike were capable of. The cries were an annoyance to the father, so much so that Mike slapped little Josh when he was just a few months old for simply crying.

After the hard smack to the face, little Josh was thrown onto the sofa as Mike ranted and raved about the boy's screaming. Cheri sat in her chair, watching it unfold. It just so happens that the family had a guest over when the abhorrent attack took place, and they went straight to social services.

A few weeks later, Josh was taken from Cheri's custody after she admitted to allowing her husband to slap their child. The little boy had an incredibly lucky escape; he ended up being adopted and was given a brand new name.

Losing custody of multiple children due to her own actions didn't faze Cheri, though. The following year, she went on to have another boy, who was quickly taken into care.

Then, in 1986, after giving birth to only boys, Cheri had a baby girl she called Maria. Her treatment of the little girl was much different from how she'd treated her sons. She ensured the girl was clean, well-dressed, and always had a full belly of food. None of her previous children had been treated this way, and it seemed as though Cheri had turned a corner this time. However, Cheri was a serial abuser. It was only a matter of time before this was discovered.

Around Easter 1986, Cheri's family was taking care of little Maria. Blood was discovered in her diaper, which had originated from her genitals. It was suspected that she'd been sexually abused, and she was taken to the doctor. The doctor called the police but still allowed Maria to go home with her mother.

It seemed as though Cheri knew what was coming. She immediately took Maria to her mother's and asked her to take care of the baby overnight. Shortly after, police officers made their way to Cheri's home and demanded to see little Maria. They couldn't because she wasn't there, the mother told them, and Cheri refused to tell them where the baby was. It didn't take long, or much investigation, to find the child at her grandmother's. The baby was taken from the family and placed into care.

However, there wasn't enough evidence to convince Cheri of abuse. Plus, some people questioned if Mike was to blame. Either way, Maria was away from the family for good and would never have to see her biological mother ever again. This had a profound effect on Cheri, who sobbed and mourned the loss of her daughter. For a while, she just couldn't accept the loss of her daughter. So, she did the only thing she could think of to console herself: have another baby.

Nine months later, Cheri Junior was brought into the world but was removed from her mother's care at six months old. Still, this wouldn't deter the woman from having more children: she had another boy named Kevin in 1991. Kevin wasn't her husband's biological child, and subsequently, she and Mike divorced.

Kevin's father, also called Kevin, would go on to marry Cheri. The couple had more children together: Zachary, Garth, and Chuck. To avoid confusion with father and son, Kevin Junior was nicknamed Punky.

Somehow, none of these children were removed from Cheri's care. As Punky grew up, he developed a cruel, violent streak, and even his mother became fearful of him. He ruled the roost, and as he developed into a young man, his aggression grew at a rapid pace. Until, in 2010, Punky was killed by a driver who'd mounted the sidewalk with their car. The young man died shortly after the collision. Cheri wasn't just upset at the death of her son; she was angry and looking for someone to blame.

Eventually, she chose Punky's girlfriend to be the target of her rage. After all, Heather, Punky's partner, was with him when he was run over. According to Cheri, she'd figured out what had happened: Heather had pushed her son in front of the car, leaving herself unscathed and causing her son to die. As the days passed, Cheri would add even more shocking details to her story, claiming Heather had paid the driver to murder her son. None of this was even close to the truth.

In reality, Punky and Heather were on their way to acquire some heroin together. The car accident, though tragic, was just that - an accident. Heather had nothing to do with it and was grieving the loss of her partner. She and Punky had a little boy together, a fact that made Cheri resent Heather. It seems Cheri only wanted to give birth to girls and despised Heather for not giving her a granddaughter.

Cheri hosted a memorial at her home, which Heather attended. However, the mother was still filled with anger and blame toward Heather, so she began whispering in relatives' ears, telling them how her son's girlfriend was to blame for his death. She spoke to Marci, a family friend, who agreed to beat Heather up.

Before she knew it, Heather was on the floor, getting punched in the face relentlessly. The woman had done nothing wrong but mourn the loss of her partner. Her only misstep was going to the memorial that day. Perhaps she was unclear as to how much Cheri had resented her, or perhaps she thought the grieving mother wouldn't cause a scene at her son's remembrance. Either way, she was wrong.

Marci dragged Heather around by her hair, pulling her outside to continue the brutal attack on the screaming woman. The family encouraged Marci to do damage to Heather, with the relatives crowding around the attack, some of them yelling, "Curb stomp her!" Marci herself was doing a lot of yelling, spitting accusations at her victim as she pummeled her. "That's what you get for messing with my family," she screamed.

By the end of the beating, Heather had a broken nose, was covered in blood, and had bruises all over her face. She was banished from the family, along with her son - Cheri's grandson.

Punky was cremated and placed in Cheri's living room. She'd place some of his belongings alongside his ashes and would often leave his favorite chocolate bars next to his urn. The woman still had three of her boys in her care - Zachary, Garth, and Chuck. Just like their big brother, they could turn violent at the drop of a hat. This worked in Cheri's favor since she had a tight grip of control over her three boys. If she wanted them to do something, they'd do it.

Cheri's desire for a little girl didn't fade as the years passed. Despite having two little girls removed from her care in the past, she still believed she was meant to have a daughter. However, Cheri was getting older, and her window for bearing another child had closed. So, she began nagging Garth to get his girlfriend pregnant.

Gina was just 15 years old when she got pregnant, and Garth proudly told his mother he was going to be a father. However, Cheri didn't want Gina to live away from the family, so she invited her to live with her, Garth, and the rest of the clan. The teenager agreed, but when she suffered a miscarriage, she had no choice but to flee the property. Cheri was enraged that the teen was no longer providing her with a grandchild.

With that plan scuppered, Cheri moved her attention to Zachary. The boy was just 13 and had no girlfriend to speak of - even if he did, she would likely be the same age as him. However, Cheri was concocting a scheme. She knew Zachary got along with a family friend, 19-year-old Vera Jo Reigle. Vera had developmental delays, so although she was classed as an adult, her mind was still that of an eight-year-old.

Cheri had known Vera her whole life, having lived in the same apartments as her parents. In fact, Cheri had babysat for a young Vera on multiple occasions, but her parents often found it hard to get the girl back from Cheri. In the end, Vera's mother had to be stern with Cheri and cease all babysitting, though they managed to stay friendly thereafter.

Vera suffered a life-changing attack at the age of 11 when her father would sexually abuse her. Her father got 20 years in jail for this disgusting crime, but Vera's life would only go on to get more tragic. Her mother would go on to meet a new man, who would also impose himself on Vera.

Despite being constantly violated and abused, the young girl grew up to be sociable, though still shy. She was keen to please, likely as a result of her abusive upbringing, which meant she was easy to take advantage of. That's exactly what Cheri Brooks had in mind. The mother commanded her son Zachary to date Vera and insisted he invite her over frequently.

Despite the boy not being overly interested in the 19-year-old - he was just 13 - he did as his mother asked. Cheri began complimenting Vera, making her feel a part of the family, and telling her she loved her. Before long, she'd managed to convince the girl to leave her mother's house and move into the Brooks household.

Dollar signs flashed before Cheri's eyes when she discovered Vera was eligible for disability checks. Soon enough, these were being paid to Cheri for "rent."

However, once the young woman was well and truly in the family fold, Cheri changed her treatment of her. Vera was forever looking to please, and the cruel matriarch made her do all of the household chores, as well as take care of Cheri, who was diabetic. The woman spent most of her time in a wheelchair due to her weight and would need washing, her bandages removed, and her feet rubbed. Should Vera do it incorrectly, she'd be whipped with a stick.

Cheri ensured Vera had no contact with her family, that her phone had been taken away, and that the teenager rarely left the house. "Your mother wants nothing to do with you," she'd spit at Vera. With Vera being so trusting, she believed everything Cheri was telling her.

By the time Zachary was 15, Cheri's plan to have him and Vera become a couple had worked. By this point, Vera was 21. It wasn't long before the young woman was pregnant - and the baby was a girl. Cheri was ecstatic. Still, her poor treatment of Vera resumed, and Cheri made sure that the mother-to-be would have no say in the upbringing of the child. She even chose the name: Willadean.

Even Zachary wasn't going to get a look in: she forced her son to sign over parental rights to her.

Cheri was born November 3 and insisted that baby Willadean have the same birthday. The only problem is that you can't decide these things, and the child wasn't due until mid-December. So, Cheri forced Vera to drink bottles of castor oil to induce labor, which it did six weeks early. Still, Willadean wasn't born until November 4, one day after Cheri's birthday. This didn't sit well with the matriarch. Still, she'd got the little girl she wanted.

With the baby being born prematurely, she had complications. Naturally, she was underweight, but she also had heart problems. All because an egomaniacal woman wanted the baby to be born on the same day she was.

As soon as Willadean was brought into the world, Cheri took over. She told Vera how to take care of the child while in hospital, and once she was discharged, the abuse resumed at home. Vera was back to taking care of the home, cleaning, and looking after Cheri. Baby Willadean was taught to call Cheri "Mommy" and spent very little time with her real mother.

If Vera tried to speak up or ask for something, she was beaten. Cheri would even command Zachary to beat her up. The young woman was never given her own plate of food to eat but rather was given the leftovers of the family's used plates. Their home wasn't fit to live in, with no running water or functioning toilet. Instead, they made use of a bucket. Still, Vera never tried to make a run for it. And, despite his mistreatment of her, Vera loved Zachary. She would show him affection and try to get his attention, though he began seeking out other girlfriends.

On several occasions, Garth and Chuck would force themselves on Vera. Nobody would bat an eyelid. It seems the whole family thought the young woman was there simply to be abused and taken advantage of.

A few years passed, and Cheri was bored of Willadean. She wanted a new little girl, not one from Vera this time. In fact, Vera was becoming a burden, and Cheri wanted her gone from the home. As a result, the beating would only intensify. Ironically, despite Cheri's disdain for Vera, she wouldn't allow her to leave.

As well as more violent beatings, Cheri also began withholding food for longer. Vera was on day three of not being fed and, in her ravenous state, ate one of the chocolate bars placed beside Punky's ashes. She knew the chocolate bar wasn't there to be eaten, and if she were caught, a violent beating would ensue. But she was desperate. However, if nobody saw Vera do it, she might get away with it. But, someone had witnessed her take the bar and devour it: Garth's ex-girlfriend Gina.

The young woman, who had fled after having a miscarriage, was back on the scene. She was doing her best to become Cheri's favorite daughter-in-law and raced back to tell her how she'd witnessed Vera taking the chocolate.

Vera was beaten relentlessly. Her nose was broken, and her face was purple with bruises after the attack. Once she'd been beaten, she was shoved into a closet. The cruel family would force Vera to eat pig waste and dig her food right out of the garbage.

Around this time, Danny Bixler arrived on the scene. He was the son of Cheri's cousin, Daniel Bixler. His girlfriend, Nicole Peters, came with him to live with Cheri while he was on the run from a police warrant. Danny and Nicola were a perfect match for one another - both cruel, sadistic, and violent. Their arrival would see the torture of Vera get even worse.

The pair would beat her and laugh the whole time, pausing to get intimate before resuming their sick attack.

In order to provoke Zachary into partaking in some of the horrific abuse, Cheri told her son that Vera was responsible for Punky's death. She announced to the whole family that Vera pushed Punky in front of the speeding car, so Zachary and Danny became full of rage and began to beat the young woman yet again. It seems they forgot that just a few years prior, Heather was the one to have supposedly pushed Punky to his death. The murderer had changed again, though Zachary or Danny didn't question this.

It's surprising that Vera was still alive by this point, let alone after that savage beating. She'd not been fed, the assaults were brutal and frequent, and her wounds were plenty. She was unable to walk properly by the beginning of March 2011.

Toward the end of March, Danny and Nicole carried out another vile attack on Vera, stabbing her in the leg. Cheri stuck her finger in the open wound. A belt with a padlock on the end became a makeshift weapon, and the family took turns swinging at Vera.

While the abuse was going on, Chuckie and Garth, along with some of their cousins, got into a fight with some other boys right outside the house. The police attended the scene but declined to enter the Brooks property. If they had, they'd have found Vera. She was feet away from being saved.

On March 26, Zachary, Danny, and Nicole marched Vera out of the house and to the railroad tracks. She went with them, hobbling to keep up with them in spite of her plethora of wounds. Once they were at the tracks, the trio resumed beating and stabbing Vera with a dull knife. They removed her clothing and continued their assault. At one point, Danny grabbed Vera from behind and dragged the knife across her neck. It was too dull to kill her; all it did was prolong the victim's suffering.

They beat her relentlessly until she was unable to move. Still alive but unable to move, they placed her on the train tracks and left. No doubt Vera knew what was coming.

When a train eventually came, it ran over Vera. However, it didn't turn her into "hamburger meat," as the group sniggered it would. With the last ounce of strength she had, Vera dragged her unclothed body to the middle of the tracks. This meant there was a few inches between her and the train passing above her. Her killers had hoped the train would destroy all incriminating evidence. They didn't bank on Vera being able to move out of its way, thus preserving the sick and depraved wounds they'd inflicted.

The train driver spotted the body, and although he was unable to stop in time, he did call the police. Their inquiry began by attending Cheri's residence. The woman said Vera's killer was likely her boyfriend. Vera had no boyfriend.

Meanwhile, an autopsy of the victim's brutalized body took place. Vera had been stabbed dozens of times. Just about every bone in her face was fractured.

Cheri's insistence that she had nothing to do with Vera's gruesome death was easily disproved by the amount of incriminating evidence found in her home. Vera's blood was all over, and there were makeshift weapons with the deceased's blood on them.

In the end, Danny and Nicole confessed to everything during police questioning. Both of them said that Cheri had given them drugs and coerced them into killing Vera. They said it was all Cheri's idea and that she wanted her dead. According to the couple, the idea of Vera dying on the train tracks was Cheri's idea.

Danny got 40 years in jail for murder, and Nicole got 23 for conspiracy. Zachary got four years in jail. Various witnesses to Vera's torture got probation and fines for obstruction of justice.

Cheri wasn't charged with murder or even conspiracy. She remains free as of writing. Willadean was removed from Cheri's custody and adopted.

A search of the murder scene found Vera's clothing scattered about. The police found her hoodie, inside which she'd written a note:

"I love you, Willadean. I am glad to be your mommy, and I am glad that I had you on Nov 4 at 4:16 am, six pounds, two ounces, nineteen inches long. Mommy loves you."

It seems Vera knew when she left the house with Zachary, Danny, and Nicole that she wouldn't be returning. She knew she was walking to her death. Perhaps, after suffering so much torture and abuse, part of the young woman had resigned herself to that fate.

The note will be given to Willadean when she's older.

Final Thoughts

Thank you for reading Unbelievable Crimes Volume Eight. Covering crimes that are lesser-known can sometimes be a hard premise to maintain. What's lesser-known in one country may be well-known in another. Similarly, one true crime follower may not have heard of a particular crime, while another knows all about it despite it being relatively unheard of.

Many of the crimes I cover are already well-known to me before writing about them, so it can be hard for me to figure out what's lesser-known in the true crime community.

I try to gauge it by the press coverage, the amount of (or lack of) documentaries or video material, and how often the case is discussed in various true crime forums. I have a spreadsheet of cases just waiting to be written up, but sometimes, I have to remove them from my list when the case gets a surge in the press or renewed interest in the case.

I hope, for the most part, I'm introducing you to crimes you'd not heard of.

If so, Volume Nine is forthcoming, and in that anthology, I've really tried to double down on the lesser-known aspect of this series. I hope to see you there!

As always, I'd like to thank you for your readership and let you know how grateful I am that you take the time to read these books. It means a lot to me and encourages me to keep writing, so thank you for being invested in this little series. I'll see you in the next one!

Take care,

Daniela

Also by Daniela Airlie

Infamous Crimes
Infamous Cults: The Life and Crimes of Cult Leaders and Their Followers

Unbelievable Crimes
Unbelievable Crimes Volume One: Macabre Yet Unknown True Crime Stories
Unbelievable Crimes Volume Two: Macabre Yet Unknown True Crime Stories
Unbelievable Crimes Volume Three: Macabre Yet Unknown True Crime Stories
Unbelievable Crimes Volume Four: Macabre Yet Unknown True Crime Stories
Unbelievable Crimes Volume Five: Macabre Yet Unknown True Crime Stories
Unbelievable Crimes Volume Six: Macabre Yet Unknown True Crime Stories
Unbelievable Crimes Volume Seven
Unbelievable Crimes Volume Eight

Unbelievable Crimes Volume Nine: Macabre Yet Unknown True Crime Stories

Printed in Great Britain
by Amazon